iPad® for Boomers

Brian Proffitt

Course Technology PTR
A part of Cengage Learning

COURSE TECHNOLOGY
CENGAGE Learning·

Australia • Brazil • Japan • Korea • Mexico • Singapore • Spain • United Kingdom • United States

COURSE TECHNOLOGY
CENGAGE Learning·

iPad® for Boomers

Brian Proffitt

Publisher and General Manager, Course Technology PTR:
Stacy L. Hiquet

Associate Director of Marketing:
Sarah Panella

Manager of Editorial Services:
Heather Talbot

Marketing Manager:
Mark Hughes

Acquisitions Editor:
Mitzi Koontz

Project and Copy Editor:
Marta Justak

Technical Reviewer:
Brown Partington

Interior Layout:
Jill Flores

Cover Designer:
Mike Tanamachi

Indexer:
Larry Sweazy

Proofreader:
Sam Garvey

For product information and technology assistance, contact us at
Cengage Learning Customer & Sales Support, 1-800-354-9706
For permission to use material from this text or product,
submit all requests online at **cengage.com/permissions**
Further permissions questions can be emailed to
permissionrequest@cengage.com

iPad, iPhone, iPod, iPod Touch, iOS, and OS X are registered trademarks or trademarks of Apple Inc. BlackBerry is a registered trademark of Research In Motion Limited. Android is a trademark of Google Inc. Microsoft, Windows, and Internet Explorer are either registered trademarks or trademarks of Microsoft Corporation in the United States and/or other countries.

All other trademarks are the property of their respective owners.

All images © Cengage Learning unless otherwise noted.

Library of Congress Control Number: 2012936596

ISBN-13: 978-1-133-94098-2

ISBN-10: 1-133-94098-6

Course Technology, a part of Cengage Learning
20 Channel Center Street
Boston, MA 02210
USA

Cengage Learning is a leading provider of customized learning solutions with office locations around the globe, including Singapore, the United Kingdom, Australia, Mexico, Brazil, and Japan. Locate your local office at: **international.cengage.com/region**

Cengage Learning products are represented in Canada by Nelson Education, Ltd. For your lifelong learning solutions, visit **courseptr.com**
Visit our corporate Web site at **cengage.com**

Printed in the United States of America
1 2 3 4 5 6 7 14 13 12

Für Elisabeth, die immer zu unserer Familie gehören wird

Acknowledgments

iPad for Boomers is the third in a series of my books about using the iPad, but in many ways it's the most important one to me. For many years I have watched older adults struggle with the nonintuitive nature of desktop computing, and I am convinced the tablet revolution currently being led by the iPad is going to be a tremendous boon to anyone who wants to harness the entertainment and learning value of these devices.

This book was completed on a very tight schedule, following the update of one of the other books in this series. My family, as always, helped me get this project completed with their constant love and support. I cannot thank the women of Team Proffitt enough—including our newest member, Elisabeth.

And then there are the professionals: great editors who have been the secret to my success. Mitzi Koontz, Marta Justak, Brown Partington, and Sam Garvey get thanks for taking my content and crafting it into something much better.

This book was unique in that it covered many different types of software applications. Several companies and developers generously donated copies of their apps so they could be reviewed and discussed. For all of the people who graciously responded to my requests for help, thank you.

About the Author

Brian Proffitt is a technology expert who blogs on ITworld.com on Open Source, Mobile, and Big Data technology and Twitters as @TheTechScribe on a wide range of technology sectors. Currently, he is an adjunct instructor at the Mendoza College of Business at the University of Notre Dame. But he won't let that go to his head.

80025 75540

Contents

Contents

Contents

Introduction

With the right applications, the iPad family of devices can become more than just content consumption devices for videos, music, and electronic books. An iPad device can help you connect with many people in your life with just the tap of a screen.

This ability to connect, given the right applications, means that the iPad is more than just some fancy electronic book or video player. It means that the iPad is an instant communications device. It is also a learning device, offering a window to the world through the Internet in a way that's easier to navigate than a standard computer.

Here are just some of the ways the iPad can help you:

* Visit with family and friends by a two-way video call using FaceTime.

* Manage your finances with powerful, easy-to-use applications.

* Find out the best ways to travel… and take *all* your favorite books with you on the road.

While a computer could handle just about all of these tasks, a laptop can be inconvenient to carry around, and the iPad's flat form greatly simplifies mobility.

Is the iPad right for everyone? That's what this book will explore. By demonstrating some of the many types of apps available for the iPad, you should be able to make the case for using the iPad yourself.

Is This Book for You?

iPad for Boomers is for anyone who wants to get started using the iPad, no matter what their age is. While we think of Baby Boomers as those people born from 1946–1963, the truth is, any adult can use this book to learn about the iPad. Think of this book as a personal tutorial, a one-on-one class with an expert user of the iPad. You get to stay in the comfort of your own home and learn how to do the following things:

* Familiarize yourself with the iPad controls and interfaces

* Connect to the Internet with the iPad using WiFi or a cellular connection

* Add apps and multimedia content to your iPad

* Communicate with friends and family via email

* Print documents from the iPad

* Use the power of Facebook to connect to family and friends

* Travel easily with the iPad

Chapter 1
First Step: Introducing the iPad

So you've heard about the iPad and are wondering if it's right for you.

The iPad device from Apple has a lot going for it, and there is little doubt that the iPad family of devices has revolutionized the consumer electronics market of the second decade of the 21st century.

In order to understand why the iPad may be a good device for you to use, it's important to clarify what the iPad is not—it's *not* just another computer. There are no keyboards, or mice, or wires to worry about. Just a one-and-a-half pound magazine-size piece of metal and glass. At first, the iPad may seem too simple to be useful, but it actually represents a kind of computing that's even easier than the computers that led the PC revolution in the late 20th century.

The reason this is happening is complicated, because like many successful products, a combination of things are involved. As the 2000s drew to a close, more and more "regular" folks were buying smartphones, discovering the advantages that corporate workers already knew: these were computers in pockets. They were even better than PCs and laptops: smartphones were and are instant-on, highly mobile devices with Internet access. What brought consumers into this market? Perhaps the most notable catalyst was the introduction of the iPad's ancestor, the original iPhone, in 2007.

With its sleek form factor, broad range of applications, and processing speed, the iPhone became a huge sales hit among consumers and business personnel alike. In that same year, Apple released what's considered to be the true predecessor to the iPad: the iPod Touch, an iPhone-like device, but without an onboard phone, that instead connected to the Internet via wireless access points (also known as *WiFi*).

Both of these devices also did something that paved the way for iPad acceptance. They introduced the concept of an on-screen keyboard to consumers and demonstrated that such a tool wasn't burdensome at all. Once on-screen keyboards became accepted, Apple knew consumers were ready for a tablet with the same kind of keyboard.

So, in 2010, Apple decided to release just such a tablet: the iPad.

In this chapter, you will explore:

* What Is the iPad?
* Choosing the Right iPad
* Getting an iPad
* Throwing in the Extras
* Setting Up the iPad

What Is the iPad?

When Steve Jobs announced the iPad in January 2010, the initial reaction was mixed at best. After the initial excitement died down, critics pointed out that this "new" device was hardly more than a giant iPod Touch. Sure, the screen was bigger, and the apps looked better, but other than that, what could such a device offer to consumers?

It turns out, plenty.

Perhaps the biggest draw to the iPad was the tablet form itself. In computer jargon, a *tablet* is any device that has a flat interface and a size that approximates a notebook tablet of paper. The size of the device is key: Digital readers such as the Amazon Kindle and Barnes & Noble Nook certainly have flat interfaces, but their smaller sizes and less robust screens put them in a different category than tablets.

The iPad features the on-screen keyboard mentioned earlier, and most applications just need your fingers to enter text and manipulate objects on the screen. With such a simple interface, and because the device itself is much lighter than laptops, notebooks, and even the ultra-light netbooks, it is a large-screen device that is much more portable for general consumers.

Besides being large enough to read comfortably (and watch the occasional movie), the screen also features a multitouch interface, which is now becoming a common experience for many electronic device users. Multitouch allows users to touch and manipulate objects on-screen with more than one finger at a time. This interface enables users to shrink objects by "pinching" them or expand object by fanning out their fingers. Or they can type capital letters onscreen by virtually holding down the Shift key on the keyboard.

Applications are the biggest key to the iPad's success, if only by sheer numbers alone. Thousands of applications are available in the Apple App Store, free or otherwise, with a high percentage of them reviewed by other users. This social review system lets you find out quickly what's really going to work—and what may not. More than that, the stunning variety of apps available makes the iPad highly suitable for any number of use cases.

Choosing the Right iPad

Before you buy an iPad, you need to figure out first which iPad you're going to get, particularly now with the release of the third-generation iPad in March of 2012. While all iPads may look alike, there are two key differences found within all iPads that make it possible to choose between a total of nine different iPad models.

When choosing an iPad device, you may find yourself gravitating toward the new iPad, which is the latest in the iPad series of devices. The good news is that from a retail standpoint, the latest iPads are no more expensive than the first iPad or the iPad 2, and each model in the respective device families is similarly priced and put together.

> **NOTE**   **An iPad by Any Other Name**
>
> Beginning in 2012, Apple decided to drop numbers from its product names for the iPad, which can be a bit confusing, since now the successive order of products is iPad, iPad 2, and (again) iPad. For most of the book, much of what will be described will apply to all the iPad devices, but if we have to point out a difference, we will call the latest device the "2012 iPad."

Key Differences Between Models

There are key differences between the first iPad, the iPad 2, and the 2012 iPad that should be taken into consideration.

First, the form factors of the iPad 2 and 2012 iPad are thinner and lighter than the original iPad. This is not a huge difference, but nonetheless it should be noted, because after holding the device for a while, you will notice the weight difference.

The three biggest differences between the devices are the following:

* The 2012 iPad has a faster processor than the other two devices in the family.
* The iPad 2 and 2012 iPad have an onboard camera.
* The 2012 iPad has a very high screen resolution that enables HD viewing.

The faster processors with each model do not change the nature of the apps that run on any version of the iPad, but they do increase the speed at which apps run on the iPad 2 and the new 2012 iPad. And the speed, like the lighter weight, is noticeable. iPad apps were never pokey, but when compared with performance on the iPad 2 and then the even faster performance of the 2012 iPad, they are indeed less responsive. Some apps, like Garage Band, can be used on the iPad, but they are recommended for the iPad 2 and 2012 iPad precisely because of their faster processors.

The cameras on the iPad 2, while not the greatest in the world, do afford the capability to run apps like FaceTime, a two-way video-conferencing app, and Photo Booth, a fun photo-morphing app. The 2012 iPad does an even better job, with a high-definition camera and an iPhoto app that will let you make edits on any picture you have on the 2012 iPad.

The one big advantage of the iPad and iPad 2 versus the 2012 iPad? Price.

While not officially sold by Apple anymore, first-generation iPads are being sold on the secondary market for big discounts from their original prices. Of course, this means that you are buying an iPad used, with all the pros and cons of such a transaction. But, if you are on a budget, picking up an iPad on eBay or some other reputable vendor would be a great way to get started.

However, Apple has decided to keep iPad 2s on the market for a while longer, and Apple is offering the devices for exactly $100 less than their 2012 counterparts.

WiFi vs. WiFi+3G/4G

The first choice point for any iPad model is whether to get a WiFi or a WiFi+3G/4G device. All iPads have the capability to connect to the Internet using wireless access—the kind found in your home or many public businesses, like the coffee shop on the corner. This is usually pretty adequate, particularly within your own home, which can easily have its own wireless network.

WiFi+3G/4G models, on the other hand, can also tap into the AT&T cellular network and connect to the Internet anywhere the iPad can receive the AT&T network. iPad 2s and the 2012 iPads can use AT&T or Verizon as a cellular carrier. The iPad 2s can connect to these carriers' 3G networks, and the 2012 iPad can connect to the much faster 4G networks on AT&T and Verizon.

You should note that WiFi+3G/4G models uniformly cost $130 more than their WiFi-only counterparts, so using a WiFi-only device is a real cost saver.

The other differentiator across iPad products is the amount of solid-state storage each device has. All iPads are currently available with 16, 32, or 64 gigabytes of storage. The price of each model is directly proportional to the amount of memory. Table 1.1 displays the retail pricing of the 2012 iPad, and Table 1.2 shows the pricing for the iPad 2.

Table 1.1 2012 iPad Pricing (March 2012)			
	16GB	32GB	64GB
iPad (WiFi)	$499	$599	$699
iPad (WiFi+4G)	$629	$729	$829

Table 1.2 iPad 2 Pricing (March 2012)			
	16GB	32GB	64GB
iPad (WiFi)	$399	$499	$599
iPad (WiFi+3G)	$529	$629	$729

NOTE

Your iPad Price May Vary

Because first-generation iPads are now only available on the secondary market, pricing on the models can vary significantly depending on the seller.

The question of how much memory you need is one that plagues most iPad device users. Understanding about bytes, gigabytes, and the like is not particularly important. What's important is knowing how many pictures, songs, and books each device can hold.

Table 1.3 puts together some numbers from Apple that do a better job of relating how big this storage is.

Table 1.3 iPad Storage Comparison			
File (Average Size)	16 GB	32 GB	64 GB
Pictures (1.5MB)	10,922	21,844	43,688
Songs (5MB)	3,276	6,552	13,104
Movies (700MB)	23	46	92
TV Shows (325MB)	50	100	200
Electronic Books (1.2MB)	13,653	27,306	54,612
Documents (50 KB)	335,544	671,088	1,342,176

Looking at Table 1.3, you might wonder why in the world you would ever need to store 1.3 million documents, and that certainly seems unlikely. But these sizes can give you a more practical idea of what kind of storage capacity we're talking about.

From a consumer standpoint, you need to factor in how you will use the device. If you are going to be based in one central location, and you plan on connecting your iPad to a PC or Mac computer on a regular basis, then you will not need a lot of storage space. You can simply use your computer (and any storage device to which the computer has access) to handle storing files. In such a case, you should probably stick with one of the 16GB models.

If, however, you plan to be more mobile or otherwise be unable to sync on a regular basis, and you will be handling a significant number of files, then consider purchasing one of the larger memory devices. It's likely that 32GB's worth of capacity is enough for most mobile use cases, unless you have a large amount of multimedia files to carry around.

One good way for travelers to pin this down is to look at the all of the files you must have while away from home, calculate the amount of memory those files need, and then triple that number. This calculation should account for the original files' storage and the potential of creating twice as many files while away from your base PC.

As for the decision on WiFi-only versus WiFi+3G/4G, here the recommendation is not strictly along financial lines. It would be easy to say, for instance, that all stationary iPad users should be fine without plunking down an extra $130 for 3G or 4G cellular connectivity. You've got WiFi set up in your home, so why bother with 3G?

This is where you should ask a key question: What happens if your Internet connection goes down? If losing Internet connectivity would harm your experience on the device, then it may be worth it to spend the extra money and get the WiFi+3G/4G model. Most of the apps in this book, however, do not require always-on Internet connectivity, so you may want to consider that, too.

The final determinate for buying a 2012 iPad or iPad 2 is color: You have a choice between a white or black screen border on these models. This is strictly a preference issue, but the choice will need to be made, nonetheless.

With these criteria in mind, you should be able to make an informed choice on getting the iPad device you need.

NOTE **When 3G or 4G May Not Be a Good Idea**

If you work in a region where AT&T or Verizon coverage is problematic or nonexistent, you may need to reconsider the 3G or 4G options. One possible workaround, for instance, would be to use a mobile WiFi device from another cellular carrier and connect to the Internet via that device's WiFi network. But, be careful: This is an expensive option.

Getting an iPad

If you are fortunate enough to live near one of the hundreds of Apple retail stores, purchasing an iPad should be a relatively painless process. Just walk in, pick out the one you want, and then take it home. As of this writing, most U.S. Apple stores had caught up with the huge demand for these devices (especially the older iPad 2s), and usually had them in stock, though it is still sporadic. You may want to call ahead and see if the model you want is in stock before driving in to purchase it.

If you don't reside near an Apple store, you have two basic options: purchase the iPad online or through an Apple partner retailer, such as Target, Wal-Mart, or Best Buy. Be careful about expecting an iPad at a retail partner, though; these stores often only get a handful of devices at a time, which are usually snatched up very quickly.

The other route you might go is to check an AT&T or Verizon retail store, but here iPads are even more scarce—only the largest stores in a given region will actually have the device in stock, while a big majority of such stores will have to order them from Apple directly.

The good news about any of these options is that the cost of the iPad, either online or at another retail store, is always the same. There's no markup when you purchase the iPad somewhere other than an Apple store, and the online store will ship iPads free of charge, so there's no additional cost there.

If you choose to visit a partner retailer, if there's one near you, you should definitely call ahead and see if there's an iPad in stock. Be sure to specify which model—you don't want to get there and find out they have models that don't meet your technical or budgetary requirements.

If you are not in a hurry to receive the iPad, ordering it online is definitely recommended. That way, you're working directly with Apple, and you won't have to dodge and weave past other shoppers to get the exact device you want.

Of course, getting a first-generation iPad is a little easier. If you find one at a reputable online vendor, you could have the device in your hands in a matter of days, at a much lower cost.

Throwing in the Extras

When you purchase an iPad device, you may be tempted by all of the nifty-looking accessories you see around you in the actual or online store. You might be tempted to try one over the other, but here are some recommendations based on consumer needs.

* **Cases.** Available from Apple and a number of third-party vendors, a carrying case is essential for anyone planning to transport the iPad device from one location to another. With a glass screen and a burnished metal exterior, the iPad device could easily be damaged without some sort of protective covering—not to mention that carrying the iPad device in full view in some public locations is an invitation to theft.

* **Smart Cover.** While not a full cover, Smart Covers are very useful for protecting the 2012 iPad and iPad 2 screens, and when they are folded correctly, they serve as a portable stand. Magnets hold the cover in place, and also serve to turn the device off and on when the cover is used.

* **Apple iPad Camera Connection Kit.** If you plan to connect any USB camera or SD flash drive from your camera to your iPad, then this accessory is essential. The ability to transfer photos, videos, or other files to your iPad without using an iTunes-equipped computer is a real time-saver.

* **Apple iPad Dock.** This is a great stand to park your iPad in an upright position while you sync to a computer or charge the battery.

❊ **A Bluetooth-capable wireless keyboard.** Available from Apple and third-party vendors, a wireless keyboard is a very essential tool for the iPad—especially if you don't like the on-screen keyboard. You might be tempted to purchase the Apple iPad Keyboard Dock and just get all-in-one functionality. This is not recommended, because the Keyboard Dock means that your screen and keyboard are mated and any change in position between the two will be impossible. Also, if you prefer a more ergonomic keyboard, the Keyboard Dock will be ill suited for you. It's better to get the Dock and a wireless keyboard separately.

Setting Up the iPad

When the big day comes and you bring that white box home, you will be very tempted to turn the iPad on and start playing with it right away. Like all good things, you will need to put a little effort into your iPad before you can run it.

When iPads initially came on the market, they had to be connected first to a PC or Mac computer that had iTunes installed.

With iPads that have iOS 5.0 installed, you no longer need to connect the iPad to any machine; it can set itself up directly over the air.

But there is one thing you can do to help set up your iPad faster. If you don't have one already, you need an Apple account. While many iPad applications are free, you may want to purchase some applications later or use the free iCloud storage service, so it's a good idea to get your Apple account set up first.

To set up iTunes and an Apple account on any computer connected to the Internet:

1. Using any browser, visit the iTunes Web page at www.apple.com/itunes/ (see Figure 1.1).
2. Click the Free Download link. The Download page will appear.
3. Confirm the operating system you are currently running (iTunes is usually right about this) and click Download Now. The installation file will be downloaded and saved to your system.
4. Follow the normal installation procedures you use to install software on your operating system to install iTunes.

Figure 1.1

The iTunes home page.

5. After iTunes is installed and running, click the iTunes Store link in the left column of the application. The iTunes Store page will open, as shown in Figure 1.2.

Figure 1.2

The iTunes Store home page.

6. Click the Sign In link located in the upper-right corner. The account sign-in dialog box will open (see Figure 1.3).

Figure 1.3

The account sign-in dialog box.

7. Click the Create New Account button. The Welcome page will appear.

8. Click Continue. The Terms & Conditions page will appear.

9. Click the I have read… checkbox and then Continue. The Store Account page, shown in Figure 1.4, will appear.

Figure 1.4

The iTunes Store Account page.

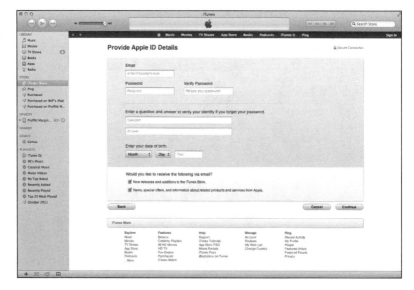

10. Enter the pertinent information and click Continue. The Payment Method page will appear.

11. Enter your credit card or iTunes gift card information, then your billing address, and click Continue. Your account will be created.

After your iTunes account (which is the same as an Apple account) is created, you will be able to set up your iPad device.

> ## NOTE   No Computer Needed
>
> There's no need to have a computer to set up the Apple account; you can sign up for an Apple account ID directly from the iPad during setup, if you like. Setting it up beforehand, however, will save you a little time come the big day.

When you first press the Sleep/Wake button along the top edge of the device, you will see the special configuration lock screen that appears only on the very first start-up. Tap and slide the gray lock switch at the bottom of the screen to begin the Setup Assistant, which starts at the language page (see Figure 1.5).

Figure 1.5

The iPad setup language page.

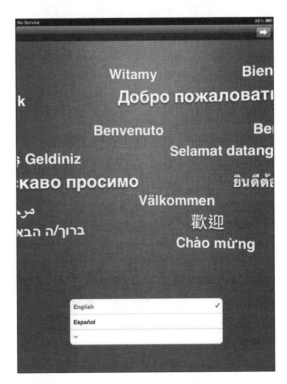

To set up the iPad:

1. Tap the desired language options and then tap the blue continue arrow. The Country or Region page will appear (see Figure 1.6).

Figure 1.6

Define your location.

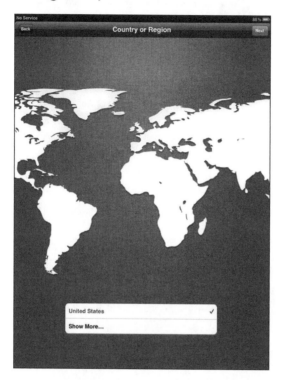

2. Tap the correct country where you reside (the iPad will make a reasonable guess) and tap Next. The Location Services screen will appear.

3. If you want your apps to always know where the iPad is, tap Enable Location Services and then tap Next. The Set Up iPad screen will appear (see Figure 1.7).

4. If this is a new iPad, tap the Set Up as New iPad option and then tap Next. The Apple ID screen will appear (see Figure 1.8).

5. Tap the Sign In with an Apple ID option. A login dialog box will appear.

6. Enter your Apple account ID and the password you set up earlier and tap OK. The Terms and Conditions page will appear.

Figure 1.7

Figure 1.7

How will you want your iPad to be set up?

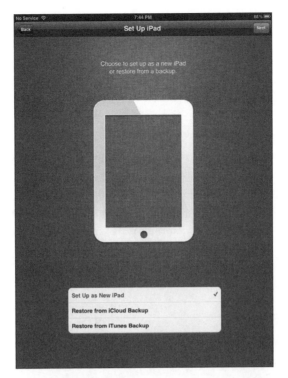

Figure 1.8

Have your Apple ID ready.

7. Read the legalese (if you want) and tap Agree. A dialog box confirming that you agree will appear.

8. Tap Agree in the dialog box. A pause screen will appear for a few moments as your ID is connected to this iPad. Then the Set Up iCloud screen will appear.

9. Since iCloud is free and we will review its operations in Chapter 15, "On the Go with the iPad," tap the Don't Use iCloud option and then click Next. The Diagnostics screen will appear.

10. Tap the Automatically Send option so your iPad will send problem reports to Apple if it ever runs into trouble. Tap Next. The Thank You screen will appear (see Figure 1.9).

Figure 1.9

You're set to go!

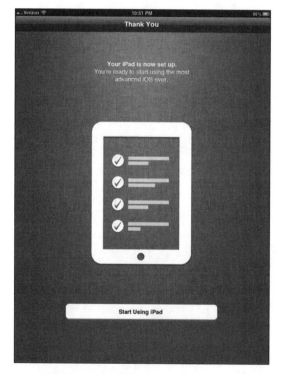

11. Tap the Start Using iPad button. The iPad will be configured to your specifications and the home screen will appear.

It is important to note that this first configuration of the iPad could take a few moments. Be patient, and everything will set up smoothly.

Conclusion

In this chapter, you learned about the origins of the iPad family of devices and why it has become so influential. You also were presented with the pros and cons of purchasing a particular iPad model. Finally, you learned how to set up iTunes, an iTunes Store Account, and the iPad itself.

While you're waiting for the iPad to finish its initial setup, grab a cup of coffee or tea and come back for Chapter 2, "Second Step: Interfacing with the iPad." There, you'll learn about all of the iPad and iPad 2 controls and even some secret control features that may come in handy later.

Chapter 2
Second Step: Interfacing with the iPad

Like most iPad customers, you may already be aware of quite a few of the iPad's capabilities. Apple's massive marketing plan has done a good job of highlighting the device so that by now most people know that the iPad is a touchscreen device, capable of connecting to the Internet and viewing a large variety of multimedia content.

When you first get to use the iPad, you will find a sleek, simple device that doesn't seem to belie that impression. A few buttons, a couple of switches—how hard can this be?

The simplicity is certainly there, but there's also a lot more going on with the iPad than you'd think. In this chapter, you will explore how to use:

* The controls of the iPad
* The touchscreen properly
* The virtual iPad keyboard
* The tools to configure the iPad

Touring the iPad Device

Take a look at the iPad. You hold in your hands a 9½ by 7½ inch, half-inch thick tablet with a grand total of four controls (not counting the screen itself, which is the iPad's main control). As you can see in Figure 2.1, three of the controls are located near the "upper-right" corner of the iPad.

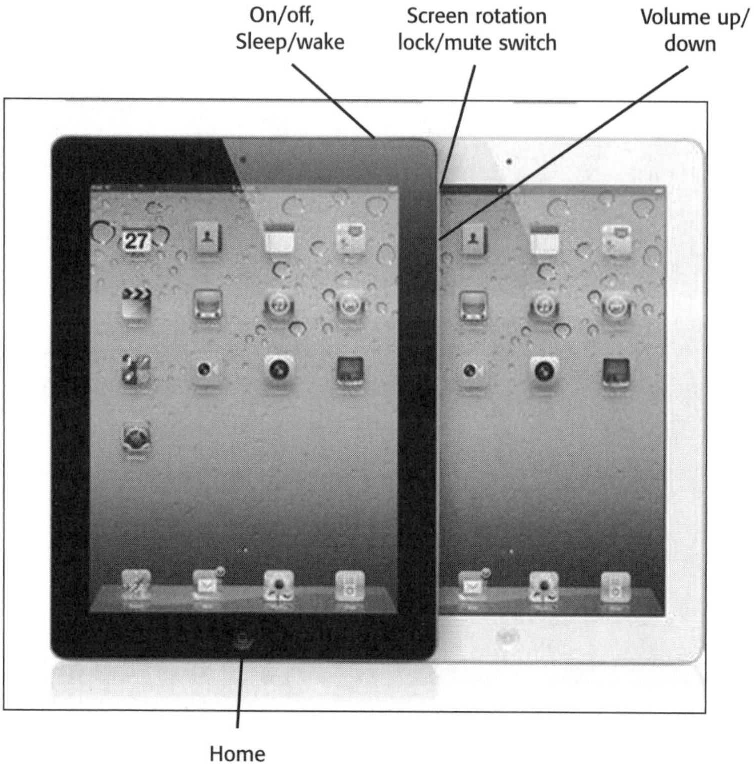

On/off,
Sleep/wake

Screen rotation
lock/mute switch

Volume up/
down

Figure 2.1

*The iPad's
minimalist
controls.*

Home

NOTE **What Is Up? What Is Down?**

The use of quotes in "upper-right" is a bit deliberate. Since
the iPad can be oriented in any direction, there really isn't a
"top" or "bottom" for the device. For the purposes of this
book, when we will actually point out the position of controls, we will assume that the iPad is oriented as shown in
Figure 2.1, with the Home button positioned at the bottom
of the device.

The control you will use the most is the Home button, located on
the front of the iPad, centered below the screen. Press the Home
button, and you will be taken immediately back to the last home
screen you were in. Since the iPad can use more than one application at a time, double-clicking the Home button will open the
App toolbar and let you switch to any other open app.

The On/off or Sleep/wake button is something you'll also use often. It has two names for a reason, because it performs two jobs. If you simply press the button quickly, it will put the iPad to sleep. It's not off, but rather in a very low-power state that will turn the screen off and prevent any other activity until the Sleep/wake button or the Home button is pressed again.

The thing to remember about sleep mode is that, while the iPad appears to be powered down, it's actually not. The device will be waiting quietly for you to pick it up and start working again, ready to pop on the instant you wake it up. To come back so quickly, the iPad is in a state of readiness that uses a little bit of power as time goes by. Very little, to be sure, but the drain on the batteries is real. Leave the iPad asleep for too long (over a day or so), and it's possible you will find the batteries very weak or even drained when you come back to wake it up.

To prevent this unfortunate surprise, you can use the same button as an On/off control. To turn the iPad completely off, press and hold the On/off button for a few seconds. A red confirmation slide control will appear at the top of the window.

To complete turning off the iPad, tap and drag the slide control to the right to power off, and the iPad will shut down. If you hold the Sleep/wake button down too long by mistake, you can tap the Cancel button on the bottom of the screen.

Once the device is all the way off, pressing and holding the On/off button is the only way to start the power-on sequence. (This is to prevent any accidental bumps from turning the iPad back on and thus draining the batteries.) It takes a few moments to cycle all the way back on, so don't worry if it seems to take a while.

The Volume up/down control, located on the right side of the iPad, does what it says. Press the top of the control to turn the volume of the iPad's speaker up, and press the bottom of the control to bring the volume down. This control is the master volume control for the iPad. Some applications, such as the Music and Video apps, have their own on-screen volume controls that handle output volume just for those apps. This is something you should be aware of, as you might see volume differences as you use different apps.

The Mute or Screen rotation lock switch is just above the Volume up/down control. Like the Sleep/wake switch, this switch also has two jobs. It may seem like this is confusing, but actually it's not. When the initial iPad was released, this switch only controlled the screen rotation—when the iPad was turned on its side, the contents of the screen were also rotated. But Steve Jobs is rumored to have insisted on making the switch a mute control, just like a similar switch on the iPhone. A software upgrade on the iPad changed the function of the switch to just mute.

That decision, however, was met with customer outcry, because many iPad users liked the screen rotation switch just fine, thank you. So, when the iPad 2 was released, Apple gave users the capability to decide for themselves. The switch can be used for one or the other function, based on a setting users can change. (You'll learn more on that later in this chapter.)

As a rotation lock, when the switch is in the up, or off, position, the screen will rotate freely based on the orientation of the device. Flip the switch to the on position, and the orientation of the screen will stay right where it is, no matter how you hold the device. This is useful, should you be reading something and don't want the contents of the screen to shift every time you move in your chair or set the iPad down.

As a mute switch, the up position enables sound, and the down position mutes the device.

There are other notable features on the iPad about which you should know. Figure 2.2 displays the top and bottom of the iPad device, where these important features can be seen. The locations of these hardware features are identical on the iPad 2 and the 2012 iPad.

Figure 2.2
Other iPad hardware features.

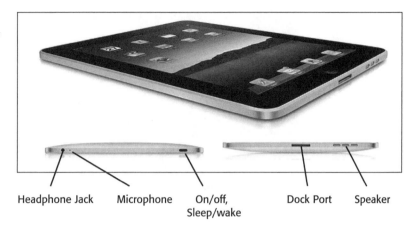

Headphone Jack   Microphone   On/off,   Dock Port   Speaker
Sleep/wake

We've already reviewed the On/off or Sleep/wake button, so here are more details about the other features:

* **Headphone Jack.** This is a standard 3.5-mm stereo headphone jack into which you can plug your favorite headphones.

* **Microphone.** This tiny hole is actually the microphone for the iPad. It does work well for everyday applications, but for higher-quality work, you may want to get a better microphone.

* **Dock Port.** This port is the primary way to connect the iPad to a PC or Mac, a power adapter, or to an iPad Dock or Keyboard Dock.

* **Speaker.** This is where the sound comes from if headphones are not in use. Try not to cover this up, so you can get better sound.

Now that we've looked at the other controls of the iPad, let's examine the most important control—the iPad screen itself. Most of the content you will view and any tasks you complete will be done on the screen, so it's a good idea to get the lay of the land.

When you press the On/off or Sleep/wake button for the first time, you will initially see the Lock screen (shown in Figure 2.3). This screen will stay visible until you slide the Slide to Unlock control or about seven seconds have passed—in which case the iPad will go back to sleep.

Figure 2.3

The iPad Lock screen.

To slide the control, place your finger on the gray arrow button and drag your finger to the right. This will open the home screen, as shown in Figure 2.4.

Here's a rundown of the different components of the home screen:

* **Status Bar.** This area on the top of the screen is home to various status messages the iPad or its apps may display.

* **Connection Status.** Displays the status of the wireless Internet (WiFi) connection the iPad is currently using. In 3G or 4G iPad models, the connectivity to AT&T or Verizon is also displayed here.

* **Clock.** Displays the current time.

* **Battery Status.** Shows the strength of the current battery charge. Also shows when the battery is being charged.

* **Apps.** Icons that, when tapped, start the various applications that run on the iPad.

Connection Status   Clock   Status Bar   Battery Status   Apps

Figure 2.4

The iPad home screen.

Favorite Apps   Home Screen Status

✳ **Home Screen Status.** Displays which home screen the iPad is currently showing and the number of available home screens. The iPad can accommodate up to 11 home screens.

✳ **Favorite Apps.** Houses your favorite apps. This area is displayed on all the home screens.

The look and feel of any of the home screens will remain the same, regardless of how many or how few apps are displayed. Each home screen can display 20 apps or folders, and the Favorites section at the bottom of the screen can hold up to six applications or folders. As you can see in Figure 2.5, the same components are visible when the iPad is in landscape mode, which is when the iPad is on its side.

Figure 2.5

The iPad home screen in landscape.

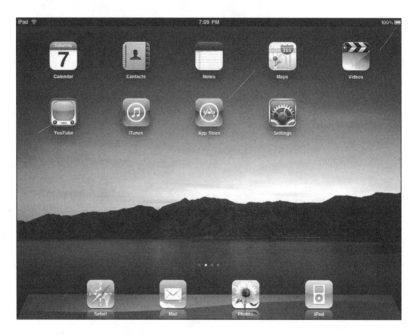

Another available screen on the iPad is the Search screen (see Figure 2.6), which is always located to the left of the home screen. The Search screen enables you to find files and applications quickly on the iPad. To get to the Search screen, swipe your finger from left to right on any Home screen until the Search screen appears.

Figure 2.6

The iPad Search screen.

Having the Right Touch

Using an iPad is not like using a "typical" PC or Mac computer, where a mouse is used to move a cursor around a screen and clicking the mouse once or twice brings up menus, windows, and dialog boxes. And perhaps, given how such actions aren't intuitive at all, this is a good thing.

Instead, the iPad has a different interface, one that makes using a computing device a lot simpler. Instead of a mouse, you simply touch the screen in certain ways, known as *gestures*.

The most useful gesture is the tap. Tapping once on the screen will start an app, "press" a button, type a key on the keyboard, or select an option on a list. The results of the tap vary from application to application, but essentially it's pressing a button.

A related gesture is the double-tap, which can also perform useful actions. In Maps, for instance, a double-tap will zoom in on the area of the map you touched. Double-tapping does not have to be very fast: two taps in one second is fast enough.

Pinching the screen on a given area can zoom out from that spot. This sounds strange when you read it, but try it, and it should make more sense. Tap the Maps app on your home screen when you get a chance and practice the pinching action. Pinching acts to bring the edges of the surrounding area "in," thus creating the zoom-out effect. The farther away your two fingers (or finger and thumb) are when starting the gesture, the more dramatic the "zoom" will be.

To get the opposite effect, you can pinch out, which is how Apple refers to the motion of starting with two fingers together on the screen and moving them apart to zoom in. This is also called "fanning," since you can fan your fingers out to achieve the zoom.

Panning, also known as dragging, is done by placing your finger on the screen and moving your finger around to display the area you want. A related move is two-fingered dragging, which will scroll any window within a window.

Swiping, as you've seen in the previous section, is done by quickly pressing and dragging a control across the screen. Swiping is also how you can move from one home screen to another.

Flicking is a similar gesture: If you have a long list of items to scroll through, flicking a finger across the screen will simulate a quick scroll with some inertia behind it.

Some on-screen objects, particularly in iWorks apps or some games, will contain objects that can be rotated. A special two-fingered move known as *rotating* will handle this. The best way to describe it is like grabbing an imaginary radio or TV knob and twisting your fingers in opposite directions to rotate the object.

Finally, some applications will need you to perform a gesture known as the long-press, also known as the "touch and hold." This gesture is pretty self-explanatory, and it can be done by pressing a part of the screen for over one second.

Keep in mind, not every application will use every gesture listed here. It varies from application to application, but these are the basic moves that will help you navigate the iPad when needed.

Typing in the Keyboard

The most noticeable lack of hardware on the iPad is, naturally, the keyboard. Like the iPhones and smartphones that are penetrating the consumer markets, the iPad relies on what's known as a *virtual keyboard* for users to enter text. "Virtual" means the keyboard is driven only by software and appears directly on the screen, as displayed in Figure 2.7.

Figure 2.7
The iPad keyboard.

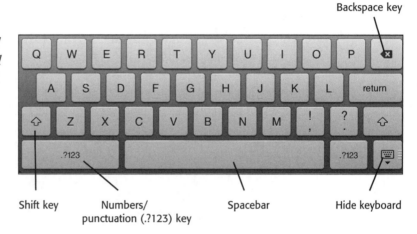

Backspace key

Shift key   Numbers/
punctuation (.?123) key   Spacebar   Hide keyboard

If you are using the iPad's Dictation feature, the keyboard will look a little different. For apps that have Dictation support, the keyboard will have a small microphone key, shown in Figure 2.8.

Figure 2.8
Taking dictation is easy.

Dictation key

Not every app will support Dictation, but if an app does, it can be a great way to enter text without typing. We will review the Dictation feature in more detail in Chapter 5, "Managing iPad Accessibility."

Keyboards appear whenever the user taps a field or an area of the screen where text needs to be entered or changed. Yes, it's "keyboards," plural, because as software, the keyboard can self-configure itself to meet the needs of the environment in which you are typing.

The keyboards in Figure 2.7 and 2.8, for instance, are the keyboards that display when using the Pages app (depending on whether Dictation is turned on). But tapping on the URL field (where Web addresses are entered) in the Safari Web browser shows some key differences (shown in Figure 2.9).

Figure 2.9

The iPad keyboard in Safari.

Note the presence of the .com key, which is a nice shortcut for typing what falls at the end of most Web addresses. The Return key has been changed to Go, and common Web address punctuation has been added to the bottom row of keys.

Because each application developer may require a different set of common keystrokes, the variations of keyboards are potentially limitless. And that's just in English (more on that in a bit).

Referring back to Figure 2.7, note the .?123 key. Tapping this key will display the numbers and punctuation keyboard, shown in Figure 2.10.

If you tap the symbols key, denoted as #+=, the symbols keyboard will appear (see Figure 2.11).

Figure 2.10

The numbers and punctuation keyboard.

Symbols (#+=) key   Main keyboard (ABC) key

Figure 2.11

The symbols keyboard.

To return to the main keyboard, tap the ABC key at any time. If you want to remove any keyboard from the screen, tap the hide keyboard key. The keyboard will be hidden until the next time you tap in a text-entry area.

Typing with the iPad keyboard is just like typing with a regular keyboard, but with some slick differences. For instance, if you find yourself typing a word that needs accented characters (such as résumé), then press and hold the "e" key and a pop-over menu containing several variations of the vowel will appear, with different accents and umlauts. Slide your finger to the correct variant (in this case, "é"), release the key, and the letter will appear in your text.

Not every key in a keyboard has these variant keys available, so you will need to explore. Two very useful variant keys include:

⁕ Hold and slide the comma key to access an apostrophe without tapping the .?123 key.

⁕ In the Internet keyboard in Safari, hold and slide the .com key to view the .org and .net variations.

Another hold-and-slide trick, which will take a little practice, is to type a letter, then slide your finger over to the .?123 key, and—without lifting your finger—slide to the number or punctuation mark you need and then let go. This will insert the character and return you right back to the ABC keyboard without having to tap the ABC key.

But the iPad keyboard has a few more surprises in store for users. Beginning with the release of the latest major update to the iPad's operating system, iOS5, the keyboard can be moved around the screen… and even split in two to enable "thumb typing."

Splitting the keyboard is very simple. Just touch the keyboard in two places and drag your fingers in opposite directions, left and right. The keyboard will immediately split, and undock from the bottom of the screen, as seen in Figure 2.12.

Figure 2.12
The split keyboard.

To move the keyboard up and down the screen, touch and drag the hide keyboard key on the right side of the keyboard, under the right Shift key. The keyboard will move to wherever is most convenient for your hands.

To merge the keyboards, just touch each side of the separate keyboard and drag the sides back together.

You can also long-press the Hide Keyboard key to view a pop-over menu that displays the Dock/Undock and Split/Merge commands (see Figure 2.13).

Figure 2.13

The keyboard control menu.

Moving Text Around

Most of us who have used computers are familiar with the word-processing capabilities of our machines when it comes to creating documents. We even take these features for granted, especially the cut, copy, and paste text functions.

But in the iPad, the question immediately becomes, how to cut, copy, or paste text without a mouse? Or a Control key?

The answer is actually quite simple, and it's just a few taps away.

To cut or copy text, double-tap the word you want to edit. The word will be selected, and an Edit menu will appear immediately above it (see Figure 2.14).

Tap Cut, and the word will immediately be removed from the document, but held in storage on the iPad's "clipboard," which is a temporary storage area for text and objects that have been cut or copied. If you tap Copy, the word will be stored on the clipboard, but not removed from the document.

Long-press the location in the document you want the cut or copied word to appear. The Edit menu will appear again. Tap Paste, and the cut or copied term will appear at the desired location.

NOTE **Clipboard Functionality**

Text or objects in the clipboard can be pasted indefinitely until another set of text or another object is cut or copied.

Figure 2.14
The Edit menu.

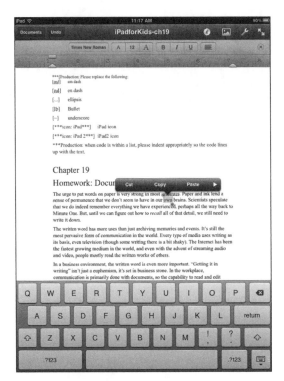

NOTE Selecting Paragraphs

To cut, copy, and paste an entire paragraph, triple-tap the paragraph to select all of it.

Configuring the iPad

Now that you have a good idea of the layout of the iPad, it's time to start customizing it to meet your personal needs. You can customize many things about the iPad, but for now we will focus on some of the more popular settings.

One of the first things users want to do is change the wallpaper on their iPad. While this seems trivial, let's face it—we all want to give things our own identifier.

To change the wallpaper:

1. Tap the Settings icon on the home screen. The Settings split view app will open, as seen in Figure 2.15.

Figure 2.15

The Settings app.

2. Tap the Brightness & Wallpaper setting. The Brightness & Wallpaper pane will open.

3. Tap the Wallpaper control. The Wallpaper pane will open (see Figure 2.16).

4. Tap the Wallpaper control again. A gallery of wallpaper options will appear.

5. Tap an image you like. The wallpaper will appear full size with an Options bar on top. You can use this wallpaper for the Lock Screen, the Home Screen, or Set Both (see Figure 2.17).

6. Tap the option you prefer. The sample wallpaper will close, and the Settings app will appear.

7. Press the Home button. The new wallpaper will be visible.

Figure 2.16

The Wallpaper pane.

Figure 2.17

Choosing where to use the wallpaper.

Users for whom English is not their native language will very likely want to make a more significant change—the addition of a keyboard more suited to their own language.

To change the language of a keyboard:

1. Tap the Settings icon on the home screen. The Settings split view app will open.
2. Tap the General settings. The General pane will open.
3. Tap the Keyboard option. The Keyboard pane will open.
4. Tap the International Keyboards option. The Keyboards pane will open.
5. Tap Add New Keyboard. The Add New Keyboard pane will open.
6. Tap an option. The option will be added to the Keyboards pane.

To use an added keyboard, enter an app that uses a keyboard. Immediately, you will see a globe key in the keyboard (see Figure 2.18). This is the International Keyboard key.

Figure 2.18

The International Keyboard key.

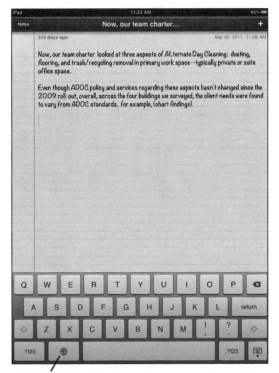

International Keyboard

To activate the new keyboard, tap the globe icon to cycle through the available options. The name of the keyboard will appear in the space-bar as you type. Or long-press the globe icon to see an action menu of the available options (see Figure 2.19). Slide your finger to the desired International option and release. The keyboard will be set.

Figure 2.19

The International Keyboard options.

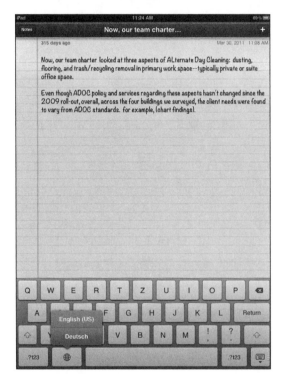

To remove an International Keyboard:

1. Tap the Settings icon on the home screen. The Settings split view app will open.
2. Tap the General settings. The General pane will open.
3. Tap the Keyboard option. The Keyboard pane will open.
4. Tap the International Keyboards option. The Keyboards pane will open.
5. Tap the Edit key. The pane will appear in Edit mode.
6. Tap the red delete icon for the keyboard you want to remove. The Delete button will appear (see Figure 2.20).
7. Tap the Delete button. The option will be removed.

Figure 2.20

Removing a keyboard.

For English users, there are additional keyboard enhancements that you may want to explore.

To explore additional keyboard options in English:

1. Tap the Settings icon on the home screen. The Settings split view app will open.

2. Tap the General settings. The General pane will open.

3. Tap the Keyboard option. The Keyboard pane will open (see Figure 2.21), and the following options will be displayed.

✻ **Auto-Capitalization.** Capitalizes the first letter after the end of a sentence.

✻ **Auto-Correction.** Displays suggested words from the iPad dictionary when iPad thinks you have made a spelling error.

✻ **Check Spelling.** Checks spelling within an open document.

✻ **Enable Caps Lock.** Starts Caps Lock typing by double-tapping the Shift key.

✻ **"." Shortcut.** Inserts a period followed by a space after double-tapping the spacebar.

Figure 2.21

General keyboard settings.

4. Select the options you want to activate or deactivate by sliding the appropriate control.

5. Press the Home button. The changes will be made.

Finally, as mentioned earlier in this chapter, you can specify whether you want the iPad's side switch to control muting the sound or locking the screen rotation.

To change the side switch action:

1. Tap the Settings icon on the home screen. The Settings app will open.

2. Tap the General settings. The General pane will open.

3. In the Use Side Switch to: section, tap the option you prefer.

4. Press the Home button. The changes will be made.

Conclusion

In this chapter, you learned about the various hardware and software controls available on the iPad. You discovered the basic gestures needed to navigate the iPad interface and learned some handy shortcuts along the way.

In Chapter 3, "Third Step: Connecting with the iPad," you'll learn how to really tap into the iPad's power by getting connected to the Internet, and you'll be that much closer to using the iPad with your family.

Chapter 3
Third Step: Connecting with the iPad

On its own, the iPad is a great device to view videos, listen to music, or edit documents. All you need to perform these and other tasks is the iPad itself. You don't even need a connection to a computer anymore.

But because the iPad doesn't need to be connected to a PC or Mac anymore to acquire this great content, it's more important than ever to be able to connect to the Internet.

Connecting to the Internet is something that can seem very daunting for many people. It seems very complicated and not a little bit risky. But Apple has taken a unique approach to Internet access: Instead of the show you everything and let you figure out what's good and bad approach, Apple gives users apps that carefully filter out content on the Internet and give you what's useful.

This is not censorship—because the Safari app is a browser that lets you see the entire Internet just as you would visit on a PC or Mac—but rather, moderation. Not only does this help protect you from accidentally treading into parts of the Internet you would prefer not to visit, but it also can give you a much richer experience and easier access to places you *do* want to visit.

For example, there's an app to visit the MSNBC website and content, and an app to visit the Fox News website and content (and CNN as well), depending on your preferred news source. There are no Web addresses to type; just tap the icon, and you're there.

But before you can access anything on the Internet, you have to establish that important Internet connection.

Besides connecting to the Internet, it's also important to connect to a more local computer, your iTunes-based PC or Mac. You don't have to do this anymore, since iPads can now perform any updates or backups over the Internet, without a computer. Still, you may find it's easier to manage your iPad with iTunes on a computer, so we will visit this topic here. Connecting to iTunes was already done in Chapter 1, "First Step: Introducing the iPad," when you first configured your iPad, but now it's time to learn more about what iTunes can do for you.

In this chapter, you will learn how to:

* Connect to and sync with iTunes
* Connect to the Internet with WiFi
* Connect to the Internet via 3G or 4G service
* Troubleshoot Internet connectivity

Connecting to iTunes

Because of the capability the iPad has to connect to the Internet, it is possible to use iTunes with the iPad just once in its operational life—right after you buy it and first start it up, as described in Chapter 1, "First Step: Introducing the iPad." Many people do this, since music, videos, and applications can all be purchased and downloaded "over the air"—which is how techies describe connections to the Internet done without wires.

For personal use only, this over-the-air approach is fine. But it is still a good idea that you connect to and synchronize your iPad with an iTunes computer on a regular basis. Even if you don't download a lot of content, connecting to iTunes will give you the very important benefit of backing up all of your iPad's data.

As nice as the iPad is, the truth is that things can (and will) go wrong. Your iPad could be dropped. Or damaged. Or lost. Even less drastic problems might happen—a poorly put-together app could freeze the iPad (which is very rare) and the only way to fix the problem might be to restore the device back to its original factory state. When that happens, having a backup of your iPad's data and settings is a great thing because you can direct iTunes to restore your apps and content and put you right back where you were before the problem started.

For this reason alone, users should regularly sync their iPad with iTunes. It's just a little free insurance.

Auto and Manual Syncing

When you connect your iPad to an iTunes computer, the process is called "synchronization" or "syncing" for short. That's because you are getting all of the content on your iPad matched up with the content on your iTunes computer.

Synchronizing the iPad with iTunes is very simple, as demonstrated in Chapter 1. Just plug one end of the USB/docking cable into the Dock port and the other end into the PC or Mac with iTunes installed. This will immediately start iTunes and begin the syncing process, as shown in Figure 3.1.

Figure 3.1

Syncing the iPad.

Depending on how long it's been since you last synced your iPad, this operation could take anywhere from one to several minutes. As it's syncing, you can still use the iPad if you want, but keep in mind that syncing will take longer if you do this.

After the sync operation is complete, you can disconnect the iPad from the computer. If you leave it connected, you can use iTunes to configure the iPad and the synchronization process.

With the iPad still connected to your iTunes-equipped computer, click the name of the iPad in the Devices section. The iPad's configuration pages will appear, as shown in Figure 3.2.

Figure 3.2

iTunes' iPad pages.

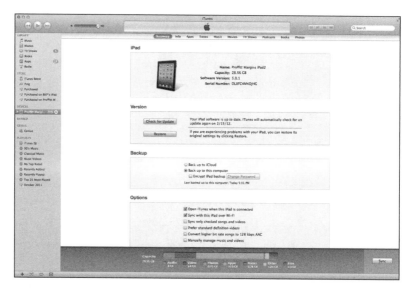

In Figure 3.2, the Summary page is displayed. This page reveals a lot of information about the status of your iPad, particularly the capacity of the device. If you are wondering if your iPad is running low on memory, this is the page to check.

NOTE Sync Over the Air

Your iPad can also be synced across a WiFi network, without plugging it in. Click the Sync button on the iPad's configuration page within iTunes, and if your iPad can be located on the local network, the Sync process will be completed without physically connecting the device to the computer.

The buttons along the top of the iPad window will navigate to other pages that will let you configure various parts of the iPad directly from within iTunes. Click the Info button, for instance, and you will find a page that will enable you to configure how the contacts, calendar, and email apps will collect their data (see Figure 3.3).

Figure 3.3

The iPad Info page.

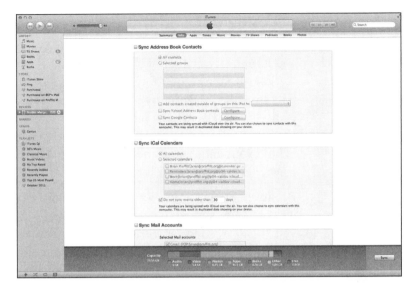

If you make any changes to your iPad configuration anywhere in iTunes, then the Sync button in the iPad window will change to two buttons: Apply and Revert (see Figure 3.4).

To sync the iPad with the new changes, click Apply.

To sync the iPad at any time, regardless of changes that may or may not have been made, simply click the Sync button in iTunes.

Figure 3.4

Applying your iPad settings changes.

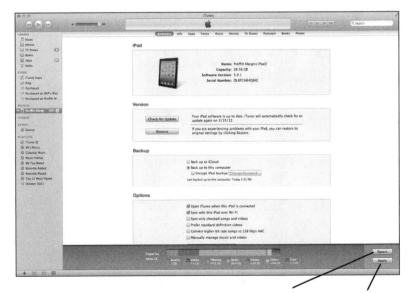

Revert button   Apply button

Choosing What to Sync

The iPad window in iTunes not only lets you configure the iPad and its apps (which will be more thoroughly reviewed in Chapter 4, "Fourth Step: Using the iPad Apps"), but it also synchronizes files from the iTunes computer to the iPad. This is important, especially if you have a very large collection of music or video files. Even at a maximum of 64GB, the iPad may not have the capacity to hold your entire multimedia collection. Or, if it does, it may not leave you enough room for apps or other data.

Because of these limitations in the memory of the iPad, you may want to keep some files on your computer only and the rest on your iPad. A good reason for doing this might be keeping your very large holiday music collection on your computer for most of the year, then swapping it onto your iPad when December rolls around… replacing your regular music.

To specify which music files will be moved to the iPad:

1. Connect your iPad to your iTunes-equipped computer, and in iTunes, click the name of the iPad in the Devices section. The iPad's Configuration window will appear.

2. Click the Music button at the top of the iPad window. The iPad Music page will appear (see Figure 3.5).

3. Click the Selected playlists, artists, albums, and genres option. The Options window will appear, as shown in Figure 3.6.

Figure 3.5

The iPad Music page.

Figure 3.6

Choose the music you want to sync.

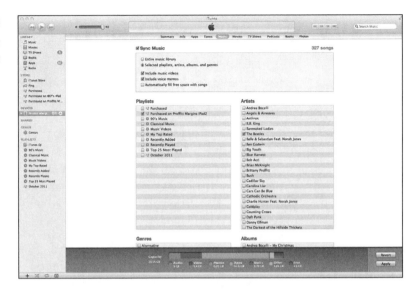

4. In the Genres window, select the option you desire.

5. Click Apply. The music on your iPad will now include only the songs in this genre (see Figure 3.7).

Figure 3.7

Chasin' those naughty blues.

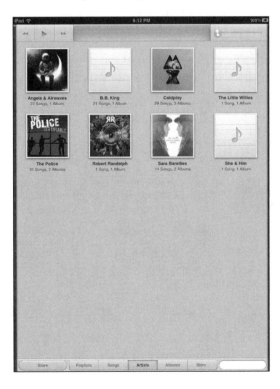

NOTE **Mixing Your iPad Music**

You can select music to sync to the iPad based on individual artists or any playlists you've created on the iPad or in iTunes.

Restoring the iPad

As mentioned earlier in this chapter, you can use iTunes to restore your iPad to either completely new factory settings (useful if you're going to sell or give away the iPad and want no personal information on the device) or to the last backup you made.

Care must be taken that you only perform a restore operation when absolutely needed. This is a last-resort solution for resolving issues with the iPad, mainly because it can take a very long time to restore the iPad.

Still, if all other options are exhausted, restoration can greatly help put your iPad to rights.

To restore your iPad:

1. Connect your iPad to your iTunes-equipped computer, and in iTunes, click the name of the iPad in the Devices section. The iPad's Configuration window will appear.

2. In the Summary window, click Restore. A confirmation dialog box will appear (see Figure 3.8).

Figure 3.8

Confirm that you want to restore the iPad.

Are you sure you want to restore the iPad "Proffitt Margins iPad2" to its factory settings? All of your media and other data will be erased.

iTunes will verify the restore with Apple. After this process is complete, you will have the option to restore your contacts, calendars, text messages and other settings.

Cancel   Restore

3. Click Restore. The confirmation dialog box will close, and the restoration process will begin.

CAUTION **Do Not Disconnect**

Do not disconnect the iPad from the iTunes computer during restoration. An incomplete restoration could create more problems on your iPad.

4. After the restoration process reaches the halfway point, you will be asked to restore the device to factory new settings or from your last backup. Click the From backup option and then click Restore.

At the end of the lengthy restoration process, your iPad should be restored to its last backed-up state.

Using the WiFi Connection

Once you have gotten the hang of connecting to iTunes, it's now time to connect your iPad to the Internet.

For iPad WiFi users, there is only one way to connect to the Internet—joining a wireless Internet network. Luckily, such networks are rather common.

Wireless Internet service works something like this: Your Internet service provider (usually the cable or telephone company) will provide a device called a router in your home. This router acts exactly like a phone. It is connected to the provider's network and from there out to the Internet. Any of your computers or other devices accessing the Internet talk to the router only, either through wired or wireless connections.

Most routers let you connect to the Internet through both wired and wireless connections, but if you are not sure, you should call the company providing your Internet service and check.

CAUTION   Getting the Right Value

If your Internet provider tries to charge you extra for wireless connectivity, refuse the charge. Most reputable providers give this service free of charge.

It is hard to know what the costs of Internet service should be for your particular area. Rural residents, unfortunately, will find it more expensive to get Internet service, because there are physical limitations in sending Internet signals over long distances. Still, the national average for Internet service is around $30 a month in the spring of 2012, so you should figure that should be your approximate price.

TIP   How Fast Do I Need?

A lot of Internet providers are going to try to sell you the fastest (and most expensive) Internet connection around. There's really no need: Even downloading a Hollywood feature film takes just 15 minutes or so on an "average" home Internet connection. Unless you are planning to download a lot of files from the Internet every day, you can save some money and go with a middle-of-the-road plan.

Once you get your wireless router, it will broadcast a radio signal at a range of about 100 yards in the clear or throughout a typical two-story home, depending on the composition of walls, layout, and so on.

One thing you need to know is that the wireless signal from your router is identified by a unique label, known as the *SSID*. The SSID is the name of the router's wireless network; think of it as the call letters of your favorite radio station. Knowing the SSID of your wireless network is important, although most of the time it will be pretty obvious what the SSID is.

That's because when devices like laptops and the iPad detect a wireless network, the device's software will also see the strength of the network and whether it's an open or protected network. If you are using your iPad in your local coffee shop, for example, you may detect a few nearby wireless networks, but if the strongest one has the SSID "Cup_O_Joe," it isn't hard to tell in this case.

CAUTION Make Sure That You Know the Network

If you are at all unsure what the right network is, do not connect to it—even if it looks right. The author was once in a major bookstore chain and noted the right SSID was accompanied by one that had a similar name, but not as strong and not protected. A little walking around found a teenager sitting in the stacks with his own router, trying to catch unsuspecting customers logging on to his network and thus have their data intercepted. If you're not sure, ask the manager.

For some networks, you may also need the key to the network. Public networks or some business networks will provide a completely open network for citizen or customer convenience. You might find the network to which you want to connect is protected (or locked) by a password, also known as a key. Before you can connect to the Internet through such a network, make sure that you have the key.

CAUTION Safety First

Unless you are on your own home wireless network, do not conduct any business or financial transactions on a wireless network—even if it's protected. Radio signals can still be received by malicious individuals and potentially decrypted. *Under no circumstances should you conduct any private business over an open network.* Ever.

So how do you know what your SSID and key are? Actually, it's not too hard: Most routers will have the information printed on a sticker attached to the side of the device. Again, if you are not sure, call your Internet provider and have them give you the information.

Once you have the SSID and key for your network in hand, you can quickly connect the iPad to the Internet.

To connect to the Internet:

1. Tap the Settings app. The Settings screen will open.
2. Tap the Wi-Fi setting. The Wi-Fi Networks pane will appear (see Figure 3.9).

Figure 3.9

The detected nearby wireless networks.

3. Tap the network you want to join. If the network is protected, the Enter Password form will appear (see Figure 3.10).

Figure 3.10

*Protected
networks will
need a
password.*

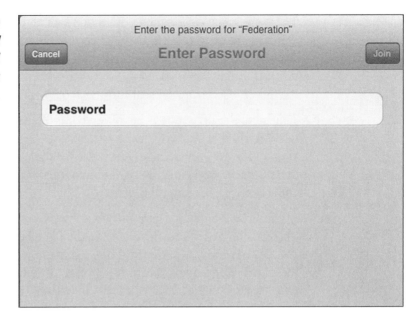

Figure 3.10

Protected networks will need a password.

4. Type the password and tap the Join key. If the password is entered correctly, the network will be joined, as indicated by the check mark next to the network name.

One great feature of the iPad is that it will remember networks as you join them. So once you join networks in various locations, the iPad will keep track of them and auto-join them when you return, so you don't have to keep remembering the passwords.

Now that you're connected to the wireless network, you can start to use any iPad application that uses Internet connectivity.

Using the Cellular Connection

iPad WiFi+3G/4G owners will have the added advantage of being able to connect to the Internet via a 3G or 4G cellular network, just like the one used by your mobile phone.

Older iPads will connect to a 3G cellular connection, while the 2012 iPad model will be able to connect to 4G (and faster) networks as well.

There are some caveats to keep in mind when deciding to use the 3G/4G connection. First, cellular connections will rarely let you work as fast as a solid WiFi connection (and 3G connections never will). If you never work away from WiFi, then don't just activate the 3G or 4G for the sake of turning it on.

That said, the very nice thing about using the iPad's cellular connection is that it's strictly pay as you go—no contracts needed. You sign up for the service, and you're set for the next 30 days. At the end of the 30 days, the plan will automatically renew, but you can cancel the plan at any time.

In the U.S., 3G and 4G are provided by two carriers, AT&T and Verizon. Verizon is only available on the iPad 2 and 2012 iPad, and you have to choose between the two carriers when you first buy these two later models. The pricing plans get a little tricky to compare, because AT&T has two payment options: up front (pre-paid) or at the end of the month (post-paid), while Verizon is paid after the month is over (post-paid). So how do they compare?

AT&T 3G service is available for the original iPad and iPad 2 and comes in one of two plans:

* 250MB for 30 days: U.S. $14.99
* 2GB for 30 days: U.S. $25

If you sign up for the 250MB plan and end up transmitting more data over the network than you planned, you will be asked to pay for the 2GB option. If you use 2GB up before the end of 30 days, you will have the opportunity to purchase one of the plans again for another 30-day period.

Under the pre-paid option, if you used 251MB in 30 days, it would cost $29.98 and 2.1GB would cost $50. But if you use post-paid, AT&T tacks on a $10/GB overage charge per gigabyte. This means 251MB would still run you about $30, but 2.1 GB would only be $35.

Just looking at AT&T alone, which original iPad users will have to do, the post-paid option is definitely better if you run over your monthly traffic limit. AT&T 3G plans include unlimited WiFi at all AT&T hotspots, too.

How does this compare to Verizon? All 3G Verizon plans, as mentioned, are post-paid at:

※ 1GB for 30 days: U.S. $20

※ 3GB for 30 days: U.S. $35

※ 5GB for 30 days: U.S. $50

※ 10GB for 30 days: U.S. $80

You can see that for just $5 more than the base AT&T plan, you can get four times the traffic allotment. Add $5 a month to the next level of AT&T, and you can get 50 percent more than the upper-level AT&T plan. If you plan on doing a lot of 3G network surfing, Verizon may be a better deal for U.S. citizens.

Canadian residents have similar plans in place through Rogers:

※ 250MB for 30 days: C $15

※ 5GB for 30 days: C $35

iPad 3G options tend to be affordable in every country where they are implemented. Note that these are plans for residents of these nations: These are not roaming charges for, say, U.S. residents traveling abroad, which are far more expensive.

NOTE   Pricing May Vary

All cellular prices were valid when this book went to press in the spring of 2012.

With the introduction of the 2012 iPad, the capability to connect to the faster 4G cellular networks for both AT&T and Verizon were added. Here, the pricing is very similar in cost and structure.

The AT&T plans for 4G are:

※ 250MB for 30 days: U.S. $14.99

※ 3GB for 30 days: U.S. $30

※ 5GB for 30 days: U.S. $50

Verizon plans for 4G are only slightly different than their 3G counterpart plans:

* 1GB for 30 days: U.S. $20
* 2GB for 30 days: U.S. $30
* 5GB for 30 days: U.S. $50
* 10GB for 30 days: U.S. $80

Again, for just $5 more than the base AT&T 4G plan, you can get four times the traffic allotment. But, for $30 a month, AT&T offers 50 percent more than the second-level Verizon plan.

So, which to choose? Again, I recommend you start at the lower end for your cellular needs. Most of the time, you won't even need the cellular connection, and unless you are pulling down a lot of big files (like movies), then 2–3GB a month is likely more than enough. Most people don't sign up for cellular access on a monthly basis, instead only using it for just the month in which they are traveling, and then not renewing it the next month when they are home.

To sign up for cellular access in the U.S., follow these steps:

1. Tap the Settings app. The Settings screen will open.
2. Tap the Cellular Data setting. The Cellular Data pane will appear (see Figure 3.11).
3. Slide the Cellular Data setting to On.
4. Tap the View Account button. The Cellular Data Account form will open (see Figure 3.12).
5. Type in the appropriate information, providing an email address and a password that you will use to log in to the cellular network.
6. Tap the desired data plan. The selection will be denoted by a check mark.
7. Enter your credit card and billing information.
8. Tap Next. The Terms of Service page will appear.
9. Read the terms and then tap Agree. A Summary page will appear.
10. Confirm your information and then tap Submit. A notification message that your account will be updated will appear. Tap OK.

Figure 3.11

Configuring cellular access.

Figure 3.12

Sign up for a data plan.

In a few moments, you will receive an Alert message indicating that your data plan has been activated. Tap OK to close the Alert box.

If you want to cancel or change your plan, return to the Settings app, tap Cellular Data, and then View Account to see the options available to you (see Figure 3.13).

Figure 3.13

You can always return to the Cellular Data Account form to change or cancel your plan.

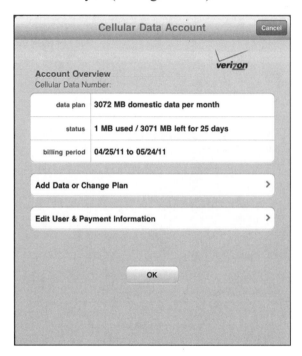

Troubleshooting Connectivity

There will be times where connectivity may not quite work as hoped. Different WiFi routers can be configured incorrectly or have some problems in the network that might limit your connection. These types of things are usually beyond your control.

But there are some things you can try if you are experiencing unexpected WiFi issues.

* **Be sure you're on the correct network.** If you have joined a network that's really far away, try joining one that's closer.

* **Look around.** If you are in a public place with lots of laptops and Internet devices going, the wireless router may simply be overworked. You may need to wait for some machines to drop off the network.

✳ **Interference is present.** Radio signals can fall victim to any kind of electromagnetic interference. Metal objects, exposed cables, microwave ovens… these can all degrade your WiFi signal.

✳ **The router dropped you.** Sometimes wireless routers can be flaky. Try tapping the Settings app, then WiFi, and then the network you're currently on. Tap Forget this Network and then follow the steps to rejoin the network.

Your iPad is pretty adaptive for WiFi conditions, so if you are having problems, it's likely the router, and not your device. If WiFi problems are consistent no matter where you try to join, it could be a hardware issue. Seek out your local Apple service specialist for help.

Conclusion

In this chapter, you found out how to connect your iPad to a local iTunes-installed computer and how iTunes can help you manage your device. You also learned how to connect to the Internet quickly and easily using WiFi access or cellular connectivity.

In Chapter 4, "Fourth Step: Using the iPad Apps," you'll delve into how iPad apps can be acquired, managed, and configured.

Chapter 4
Fourth Step: Using the iPad Apps

Since the popularity of the iPhone, you may have heard the advertising catch phrase "there's an app for that," which has become synonymous with the iPhone and now the iPad. From games to productivity to content—with the thousands of apps available, and more coming every day, there almost is an app out there for anything you might want to do.

As part of the "walled garden" approach that Apple has toward content, all applications for the iPad are only available through the iTunes Store. This central-store method means that ideally all applications will be checked for stability, appropriateness, and malicious behavior before they are ever made available to you.

And there is also a system of customer feedback on the App Store, where users like you are able to quickly rank applications based on a five-star system, as well as provide detailed reviews on what they like (and don't like) about an app. This review system is a great way to narrow down the quality applications for your iPad.

In this chapter, you will discover how to:

* Open and rearrange apps on your home screen
* Switch between apps
* Close apps that are having problems
* Download free and purchase commercial apps from iTunes
* Configure app settings
* Remove an app from the iPad

Opening and Arranging Apps

Apps come in all shapes and sizes, but they all share a common feature: How they are started. From any home screen, just tap the app's icon once. No matter what app you are using, that one action will always get the application started.

The presentation of app icons on the home screens is initially determined by the iPad, but you can quickly shuffle them around to any configuration you want.

To move app icons, long-press any icon on any home screen. In a brief moment, you will see the icons start to shake in their positions (see Figure 4.1).

Figure 4.1

Shaky apps, ready to move.

Look again at Figure 4.1, and you will note that some apps now have black X icons. These are apps that can be removed from the iPad. Note that in this picture, some of the apps in the Favorites area cannot be removed. That's because they are system apps, put on the iPad by Apple, and are not able to be removed.

Regardless of their removability, *all* apps can be moved to any part of the screen.

To move an app to a different screen location:

1. Long-press any icon on the home screen. The icons will begin to shake.
2. Tap and drag the icon you want to move to another part of the home screen.
3. Click the Home button. The apps will stabilize, and the app will reside in its new position.

Moving an app icon to another home screen is just as easy. In fact, when you long-press an icon, notice the home screen status indicator (which is the row of dots near the bottom of the screen). It will add another home screen dot to your collection as a potential destination for any moved app. If you don't make use of the empty home screen, the home screen indicator will display the same number of screens you had before the move operation.

To move an app to another home screen:

1. Long-press any icon on the home screen. The icons will begin to shake.
2. Tap and drag the icon you want to move toward the edge of the home screen, adjacent to the home screen to which you want to move the icon. After a pause, the next home screen will slide into view.
3. Drag the app icon to the desired spot on its new home screen.
4. Click the Home button. The apps will stabilize, and the app will reside in its new position.

You can also store apps within folders on the iPad screen. This feature lets you store more apps on a particular screen and, even better, organize your apps into something that makes a bit more sense. For instance, if multiple children are using the iPad, you can store each child's set of apps within a folder with their name, so the apps are easy to locate and use.

To create a new folder and name it:

1. Long-press any icon on the home screen. The icons will begin to shake.

2. Tap and drag the icon you want to store in a folder so it is on top of another icon you want to store in the same folder. After a pause, the icons will superimpose, and a new folder pop-over window will appear (see Figure 4.2).

3. Drag the app icon to the desired spot within the folder window, as seen in Figure 4.3.

4. The iPad will attempt to guess at a suitable folder name, but if it needs to be changed, tap the name field and use the keyboard to enter a new name.

5. Tap Done on the keyboard and then click the Home button. The Folder will be renamed, as seen in Figure 4.4.

Folders, like app icons, can be moved around to any iPad location, including the Favorites area, located on the bottom of every home screen. The Favorites area will house up to six app icons or folders. Move any icon to the Favorites by long-pressing it and dragging it to the Favorites area.

Figure 4.3

Positioning apps in the folder window.

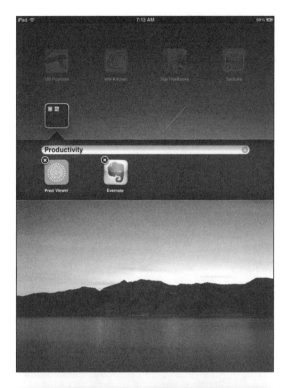

Figure 4.4

A new folder, set and named.

You can also, should you want, use iTunes to move your app icons or folders around. This is especially useful if you want to do a lot of reorganizing.

To move apps with iTunes:

1. With the iPad connected to your iTunes-equipped computer, and with the mouse, click the name of the iPad in the Devices section. The iPad's Configuration window will appear.

2. Click the Apps button near the top of the window. The Apps page will be displayed (see Figure 4.5).

Figure 4.5

The iTunes Apps configuration page.

3. Click the home screen you want to modify. The home screen will appear.

4. Click the app or folder icon you want to move. The icon will be selected, and the X icon will appear.

TIP   Move More Than One Icon at a Time

To select multiple icons, hold the Ctrl key on your keyboard and click the mouse on each icon.

5. Click and drag the icon(s) to the destination home screen.

6. Click and drag individual icons to the desired locations on the new home screen.

7. Click Apply. The iPad will be synced with the new changes in place.

Acquiring Apps

Getting apps for the iPad, whether free of charge or something for which you pay, is always done through the iTunes Store. Fortunately, you can get to the iTunes Store through the iTunes application on your computer or "over the air" using the App Store app on your iPad.

The real trick to getting an app for your iPad is finding the right one. While Apple has tested the apps in the App Store and found them to be free of viruses and relatively stable, don't assume that every app in the App Store will be the greatest thing since sliced bread, even if it's in a featured spot within the App Store.

When you hear about a new app on the Internet, read more than one review about the app from reputable sources. Use your favorite search engine to locate such reviews or blog entries about the app.

If you still want to try the app, or you're looking for apps in the App Store itself, the next place to check is the review section of the app itself. Look at the number of positive versus negative ratings, but also read the reviews. Sometimes disgruntled users will blast an app for some feature (or lack of feature) you don't even need. "It won't scramble eggs!," they cry. Okay, that's notable, but you're just looking for an app to help you garden, so the lack of scrambled eggs is not a problem.

If there is a free version of the application available, you should definitely try that one first. It may have limited features, but it should give you a feel for how the app is put together and if (with the added features) the paid version will be a good fit.

One thing to watch out for is the iPhone apps that can run on the iPad. iPhone apps can be made to run on the iPad, but such quick changes will result in an application that's clearly not configured for the iPad (see Figure 4.6).

Figure 4.6

*Google Plus:
Great social
media app,
but not quite
ready for the
iPad.*

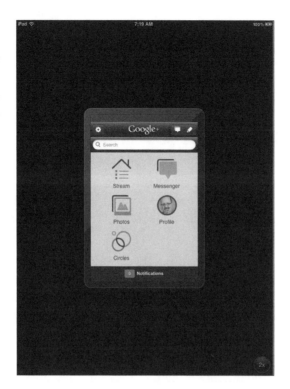

Figure 4.7 displays what happens when you tap the 2X button in one of these iPhone-only apps. More readable, but still not great quality. For this particular app, the issue is not a major concern, but this kind of scrunched-up screen in iPhone-only apps can be a little off-putting.

You may like the app so much that you will live with this configuration (at least until the developers come out with a true iPad version). One way to know if you are getting an app like this is to look for a small "+" symbol in the app's download button. This symbol indicates that the app was developed for the iPad *and* the iPhone. Also, look at the screenshot of the app on the app's download page in the App Store—this will give you an idea of what the app will look like on your iPad.

Each version of the App Store (whether in iTunes or the App Store app) will have different categories to organize apps. Most of these categories overlap, but if you are having trouble finding something, try browsing both stores.

Figure 4.7

Google Plus in 2X view.

Finally, the Search bar in both versions of the App Store is a powerful tool for locating apps. This tool will search app titles, keywords, and descriptions to help you find the appropriate application.

Given all of these avenues, you should be able to find the app you want. Now, let's find out how that's done.

Using the iTunes Application

Though the content of the iTunes version of the App Store is identical to its iPad counterpart, the iTunes application is best to use when you are planning on finding and installing a lot of apps. It's not a question of speed, but rather organization. You can find, download, and install apps with the iTunes application and then use the same application to quickly organize the apps on your iPad.

To use the iTunes application to find the popular Netflix app:

1. Start iTunes on your PC or Mac; then click the iTunes Store link. The iTunes Store window will appear.

2. Click the App Store tab. The App Store window will appear.

3. Click the iPad button to shift the App Store to iPad apps (see Figure 4.8).

Figure 4.8

The iPad section of the App Store in iTunes.

4. Click in the Search Store field, type Netflix, and press Enter. The results will be displayed, as shown in Figure 4.9.

Netflix app

Figure 4.9

Tracking down Netflix.

5. Click the Netflix app. The Netflix app page will open (see Figure 4.10).

Figure 4.10

The Netflix app page.

6. To read more about the app, click the More link below the Description paragraph.

7. To find out how other users liked the app, read the Customer Ratings section.

8. When satisfied you want to download this app, click the Free App button. A login dialog box will appear (see Figure 4.11).

Figure 4.11

You must log into the iTunes Store for every app, even the free ones.

9. Enter your ID and Password information for the iTunes Store and click Get. The app will be downloaded.

10. The next time you sync with the iPad, the new app will be loaded onto the iPad.

TIP

Redeem Your Gift Cards

If you have an iTunes Gift Card or Gift Certificate, click the Redeem link on the home page of the iTunes Store; then provide your gift card information. If you purchase an app, you will be given the choice to use the redeemed gift card amount or the payment method associated with your iTunes account.

Using the App Store App

Finding and installing an app from the iPad is just as easy as using the iTunes application. Let's track down the Silver Surf app, which is a great app to set up your iPad to be more user-friendly if you have vision issues. (We'll go over Silver Surf in more detail in Chapter 5, "Managing iPad Accessibility.")

To use the App Store app to find the Silver Surf app:

1. Tap the App Store icon to start the App Store (see Figure 4.12).

Figure 4.12
The App Store app.

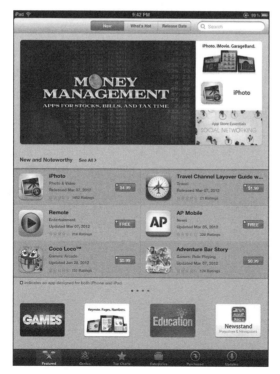

2. Tap the Search bar, type Silver Surf, and tap Search. The results will be displayed, as shown in Figure 4.13.

Silver Surf app

Figure 4.13

Tracking down Silver Surf.

3. Tap the Silver Surf app. The Silver Surf app page will open (see Figure 4.14).

4. To read more about the app, tap the More link below the Description paragraph.

5. To find out how other users liked the app, read the Customer Ratings section.

6. When satisfied you want to download this app, tap the Free button below the large app icon. The button will change to a green Install App button.

7. Tap the Install App button. A login dialog box will appear.

8. Enter your iTunes Password information for the iTunes Store and tap OK. The app will be downloaded and installed.

Figure 4.14

The Silver Surf app page.

Updating Apps

As improvements and fixes are made to the applications installed on your iPad, the App Store will keep track of any new versions for your installed software, and when they arrive, the App Store app will notify you with a red numeric indicator on the App Store icon (see Figure 4.15).

To update an app:

1. When an indicator number is visible, tap the App Store icon. The App Store will open.

2. Tap the Updates icon on the tab bar. The Updates page will open.

3. Tap the Update All button. The App Store will close, and any apps in the Updates list will be downloaded and installed.

Numeric indicator

Figure 4.15

The number indicates the number of apps to be updated.

Configuring Apps

Applications in the iPad vary in how they can be configured. Some apps have just a few configuration settings, if any, so the tools to configure them will be found in the App itself.

But some iPad apps will follow iPad convention and plug their configuration settings in the iPad Settings app. If you can't find configuration settings in your app, check the Settings app. For this example, let's configure the iBooks app, which will let you read books on the go. (We'll review the iBooks app in Chapter 9, "iBooks for Reading.")

To configure iBooks settings:

1. Tap the Settings app icon. The Settings app will open.
2. Tap the iBooks setting. The iBooks setting pane will open on the right side of the screen (see Figure 4.16).

Figure 4.16

An example of an app's configuration settings.

3. Slide the settings switch you would like to change in iBooks. The setting will be activated or turned off.

4. When your configuration is complete, click the Home button. The settings change will be made in iBooks.

Removing Apps

If you find you're not using an app, you can easily opt to remove it from your iPad. In this example, let's remove the Netflix app because you're too busy working to use this cool service.

To remove an app:

1. Long-press the app you would like to remove. The apps will begin to shake, and removable apps will be indicated by a black X indicator.

2. Tap the Netflix app. A confirmation dialog box will appear (see Figure 4.17).

Figure 4.17

Confirm you want to delete an app.

3. Tap Delete. The app will be removed from your screen.

4. Click the Home button. The app icons will stabilize.

> **NOTE** **Gone, but Not Forgotten**
>
> When an app is removed from the iPad, it will still be maintained in the iTunes Library on your computer. To completely remove the app, click the Apps link in iTunes, select the app, and press Delete. You will be asked to confirm the action and whether or not you want to keep the app's files or move them to the Recycle Bin. Select the option you want, and the app will be completely removed from your Library.

Conclusion

In this chapter, you've learned how to acquire, manage, and configure new apps for the iPad.

In Chapter 5, "Managing iPad Accessibility," you'll discover how to make the iPad a more helpful device for your personal needs.

Chapter 5
Managing iPad Accessibility

As the years roll past, it's a fact of life that some of us will experience a dampening of the senses that we once enjoyed. Medical advances are doing wonders, but the simple truth is, we may not be seeing as clearly or hearing as well as we approach the silver years.

The iPad is regarded as a highly accessible device, which is good news for anyone who needs a little help with his vision or hearing, or with physically controlling the device. In this chapter, you will explore the following accessibility features:

❋ Physical aids such as Dictation and AssistiveTouch

❋ Tools to help those with vision concerns, like VoiceOver

❋ Audio-assist tools like Mono Audio

Accessing the iPad

If you are having difficulty typing or otherwise touching the various elements on the iPad screen, the iPad has two great tools to help you: Dictation and AssistiveTouch.

As we mentioned in Chapter 2, "Second Step: Interfacing with the iPad," Dictation is an iPad feature that enables you to speak into the iPad microphone and enter your text into an app without typing a thing. You may have enabled Dictation during the setup process for the iPad, but just in case you didn't, it's simple enough to turn on.

To start Dictation:

1. Tap the Settings app. The Settings app will open.

2. Tap the General option on the left pane of the screen. The General settings will appear in the right pane.

3. Scroll down toward the bottom of the screen and tap the Keyboard option. The Keyboard settings will appear (see Figure 5.1).

4. Slide the Dictation switch to On. An Enable Dictation dialog box will appear.

5. Tap Enable. Dictation will now be active.

Not every app will support Dictation, but if an app does, it can be a great way to enter text with typing. You will know if an app is Dictation-ready by the appearance of the little microphone key on the keyboard.

To use Dictation:

1. Tap the Dictation key and speak normally into the iPad microphone near the top of the screen.

2. Tap the Dictation key again. After a few seconds, your words will be transcribed on the screen.

That's all there is to it. You will find that this will be true of all of the iPad's accessibility tools. They are very simple to use, because otherwise it would defeat the whole point of using them, wouldn't it?

Dictation is a good tool, and it typically gets better with time. It's not foolproof, however. You should re-read what Dictation puts on the screen, in case it made a mistake. If it has, you will either need to fix the error using the keyboard or erase the text and try again with Dictation.

If you have even more difficulty in using the controls and gestures within the iPad, you can use the AssistiveTouch features to simplify the way you use the iPad.

AssistiveTouch has two main purposes: to provide alternative ways to interact with the iPad in case one of its components (such as the Home button) is not working properly or to make it a lot easier to duplicate iPad gestures with just a single finger or assistive device.

To activate AssistiveTouch:

1. Tap the Settings app. The Settings app will open.
2. Tap the General option on the left pane of the screen. The General settings will appear in the right pane.
3. Tap the Accessibility option on the right pane. The Accessibility screen will appear, as seen in Figure 5.2.
4. Tap the AssistiveTouch option. The AssistiveTouch screen will appear.
5. Slide the AssistiveTouch control to On. The feature will be activated, which will be indicated by the presence of a new button in the lower-right corner of the screen (see Figure 5.3).
6. Tap and drag the AssistiveTouch control to one of the eight positions on the screen that you prefer.

Once AssistiveTouch is activated, you can use it to control your iPad with just a single finger or assistive device.

Figure 5.2

iPad's Accessibility settings.

Figure 5.3

The Assistive Touch control.

AssistiveTouch

To use AssistiveTouch:

1. Tap the AssistiveTouch control. The main AssistiveTouch menu will appear in the middle of the home screen, as seen in Figure 5.4.

Figure 5.4

The Assistive Touch menu.

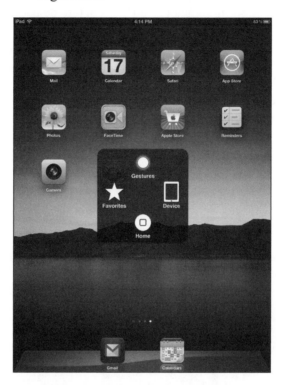

2. Tap the Device icon. The Device menu will open (see Figure 5.5).

Figure 5.5

Controlling the device.

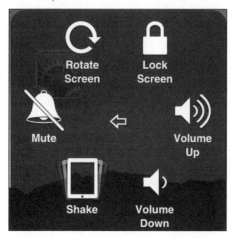

3. To use any one of these controls, simply tap it. For screen rotation, tap the Rotate Screen option. The Rotate menu will appear.

4. Tap one of the options to rotate the screen to how you need it.

5. To return to the previous menu, tap the back arrow in the center of the menu.

6. To close the AssistiveTouch menus, tap anywhere else on the screen.

One of the nice features about AssistiveTouch is its capability to mimic multifinger gestures with just a single finger.

To use AssistiveTouch to perform a gesture:

1. Tap the AssistiveTouch control. The main AssistiveTouch menu will appear in the middle of the home screen.

2. Tap the Gestures icon. The Gestures menu will open (see Figure 5.6).

Figure 5.6

Select a gesture.

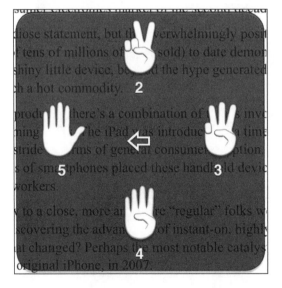

3. Tap the gesture you need to use. The gesture indicator will appear as blue circles on your screen.

4. With just one finger, tap and drag the screen. The app will react just as it would if you were using the number of fingers you selected in the Gestures menu.

5. Tap the AssistiveTouch control to turn off the gesture indicators.

If there is a particular gesture you find yourself making a lot, AssistiveTouch will let you record a gesture of your own.

To record a gesture in AssistiveTouch:

1. Tap the AssistiveTouch control. The main AssistiveTouch menu will appear in the middle of the home screen.

2. Tap the Favorites icon. The Favorites menu will open (see Figure 5.7).

Figure 5.7

All your favorite gestures.

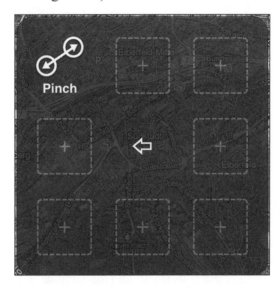

3. Tap one of the empty squares to start adding a new gesture. The New Gesture screen will appear (see Figure 5.8).

4. Perform the gesture on the screen (or have someone help you do it). AssistiveTouch will automatically start recording the gesture.

5. Tap the Stop button. The gesture will be recorded.

6. Tap Save. The New Gesture dialog box will appear.

7. Type a name for the gesture and tap Save. The new gesture will appear in the Favorites menu and in the Settings app under AssistiveTouch's settings.

Figure 5.8

Record a gesture.

As you can see, AssistiveTouch and Dictation can alleviate a lot of problems for anyone who has motor control concerns. With a little practice, these controls can let you navigate the iPad like a pro.

Seeing the iPad

Since the iPad is a very visual device, it only makes sense that the popular tablet will integrate many features to assist people with vision problems.

Perhaps the most comprehensive vision-oriented accessibility feature is VoiceOver, which essentially can read virtually everything on the screen to you. That's a simple-sounding feature, but in order to work on the iPad, it means implementing some changes in the way that gestures are used to navigate within applications.

To start VoiceOver:

1. Tap the Settings app. The Settings app will open.

2. Tap the General option on the left pane of the screen. The General settings will appear in the right pane.

3. Tap the Accessibility option on the right pane. The Accessibility screen will appear.

4. Tap the VoiceOver option. The VoiceOver screen will appear (see Figure 5.9).

Figure 5.9

VoiceOver settings.

5. Slide the VoiceOver control to On. The feature will be activated.

It is very important to understand that once the VoiceOver feature is turned on, the way you interact with the iPad screen is going to change significantly. That's because once you tap a button or option on the screen, VoiceOver is going to read that button to you first.

For gestures, what this means is that instead of a single tap to activate a button or other object, you will need to tap the control once to hear what it is and then double-tap the control to actually make it do what you want. To scroll anything on the screen, you will need to use three fingers instead of one in order to skip the reading functionality.

This takes quite a bit of practice, so it's good that there's a VoiceOver Practice button in the VoiceOver settings to deliver the practice. Tap this button (using the tap, double-tap gesture) and practice these gestures:

* **Touch.** Selects item under your finger.
* **Flick left.** Moves to previous item.
* **Flick right.** Moves to next item.
* **Double-tap.** Activates the selected item.
* **Two-finger single tap.** Pauses or continues speech.
* **Two-finger scrub (dragging).** Activates a Back button if present
* **Two-finger flick up.** Reads page starting at the top.
* **Two-finger flick down.** Reads page starting at selected item.
* **Three-finger single tap.** Speaks page number or rows being displayed.
* **Three-finger flick up.** Scrolls down one page.
* **Three-finger flick down.** Scrolls up one page.
* **Rotate clockwise.** Selects next rotor setting.
* **Rotate counterclockwise.** Selects previous rotor setting.
* **Pinch close.** Unselects text.
* **Pinch open (fan).** Selects text.

It's quite a bit to practice, but well worth it if you need the VoiceOver help.

One gesture that might need explanation is the rotate gesture, which involves simply taking two fingers and turning them on the screen as you would a TV or radio knob (remember those?). This gesture brings up the Rotor control, which lets you choose between characters, word, lines, etc. when you flick between items.

Another important control is the Speaking Rate control. If you find VoiceOver is going too slowly or too fast, you can change the rate at which VoiceOver reads by tapping and sliding this control to find the right rate.

There are several other visually oriented tools in the iPad's tool belt that can help you. All of them are located in the Accessibility settings of the Settings app.

Zoom, for instance, will magnify the entire screen when you perform a three-fingered double-tap. A three-fingered drag will move the view around the screen, and if you perform a three-finger double-tap and then (still with three fingers) move up or down the screen, you can control the amount of zoom.

Large Text enables you to set the text for the Apple apps that came with your iPad to be much larger, depending on your needs. Tap this setting, and you can set the text size as large as you want (see Figure 5.10).

Figure 5.10

Large Text settings.

If you have trouble with distinguishing contrast between items, a great way to quickly increase the contrast of the iPad screen is to activate the White on Black feature. This will immediately reverse every color on the screen, which looks unusual, but may make things easier to read (see Figure 5.11).

Figure 5.11

Achieving high contrast.

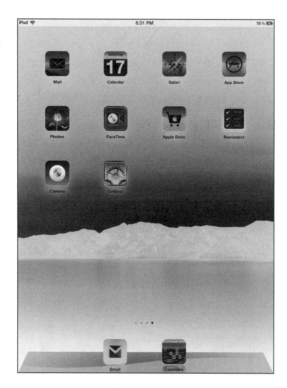

If any of these features sounds appealing, but you are sharing the iPad with someone who might not want them, you can tie the activation of these features to a unique action: triple-clicking the Home button.

To connect an accessibility feature to the Home button:

1. Tap the Settings app. The Settings app will open.

2. Tap the General option on the left pane of the screen. The General settings will appear in the right pane.

3. Tap the Accessibility option on the right pane. The Accessibility screen will appear.

4. Tap the Triple-click Home button. The Triple-click Home page will appear.

5. Tap the option you want to assign to the Home button. The feature is assigned.

Now, when you triple-click the Home button, that feature you need will be turned on or off.

Hearing the iPad

For the hearing impaired, the iPad has several ways to help. First, the headphone and Bluetooth features will let you plug in your own hearing devices so you can concentrate on the sound and eliminate background noise.

You can also use the Mono Audio setting in the Accessibility screen to shift the sound output from one speaker to the other, if your hearing is better in one ear.

Conclusion

In this chapter, you learned about the various accessibility features available on the iPad. With some practice, you can master the iPad despite any physical challenges you might face.

In Chapter 6, "Work the Web: Safari," you'll use your iPad to start getting out to the Internet, and see what there is to see on the vast network known as the Web.

Chapter 6
Work the Web: Safari

Remember when browsing was something you just did in a store and told the salesperson so they'd leave you be?

Today, browsing has a much different meaning. When the Internet was first made available for public use in 1993, the technical people who first used the part of the Internet known as the World Wide Web (now called just the Web) began calling information on the Web *pages* and calling the process of reading those pages *browsing*. That's where the term *browser* name comes from: an application that enables browsing on the Web.

Later, when even more people started using the Web, the verb *browsing* got changed into *surfing*. The name *browser* stuck, though, because it still describes more accurately what this type of application does.

As the Web grew more popular, many people—businesses, civic organizations, places of worship—were quick to see the value of the Web. It's a great way to communicate more robustly with customers and members.

In this chapter, you will find out how to:

❋ Navigate websites
❋ Manage bookmarks and history
❋ Use multipage browsing
❋ Search for content
❋ Customize your browser experience

Navigating Websites

Browsing is more than just tapping through a collection of files. What really makes the whole thing work is the Uniform Resource Locater (URL), which is what you and I would call the Web page address. Like area codes and phone numbers, URLs are pseudo-English labels that make it possible to find and retrieve any page on the Internet in a consistent, predictable, well-defined manner. URLs make it easy for regular folks to type an address into the Address Bar of Safari and bring up a page.

Of course, when you see URLs that look like http://www.apple.com, you might wonder how simple this is. But here's a quick explanation.

* **http://:** This bit of text stands for HyperText Transport Protocol, which is a technical piece of information the browser needs so that it knows that you are looking for something on the Web, and not another part of the Internet.

* **www:** Many sites don't need this anymore, but this is a formal way of calling up a page on the World Wide Web.

* **apple:** This is a proper name of the website or the company or organization the website represents (in this case, the Apple company).

* **.com:** The "dot something" that ends any Internet address. .com (for commercial sites) is the most common ending on URLs, but there is also .net and .org for non-commercial sites, .edu for schools and institutions of higher education, and .gov for government sites. Countries have their own suffixes, too: Germany has .de; France, .fr; and the United Kingdom, well, .uk, of course.

NOTE **Dot? Who's Dot?**

The period in all Internet addresses is pronounced "dot." The / symbol is called "slash."

You can begin browsing with Safari as soon as you start the app. If the iPad is not connected to the Internet yet, Safari will prompt you to make that connection.

To start browsing with Safari:

1. Tap the Safari icon. Safari will start (as shown in Figure 6.1).

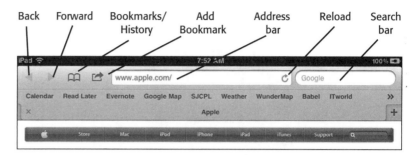

Figure 6.1

The Safari browser.

2. Tap the Address bar and then the clear field icon so the URL in the field is removed and the keyboard appears.

3. Type the URL for the website you want to visit in the Address bar.

NOTE **A Helping URL Hand**

You do not have to type the URL identifier http:// before the website address. Safari will fill it in for you.

4. Tap Go to visit the new page.

5. Long-press a highlighted or underlined hyperlink. An action menu will appear, giving you the options to open the link, open the link in a new tab, add the link to your browser's Reading List, or copy the link (see Figure 6.2).

6. Tap Open to go to the new page.

You don't have to type in the full address every time you visit a website, thanks to the AutoFill feature in the Address bar. Just start typing the URL, and Safari will display a list of similar URLs for you to choose from.

Figure 6.2

A hyperlink action menu.

After you have been browsing for a while, you may need to go back to a Web page you visited earlier in your current browser session. Two controls, the Back and Forward buttons, will enable you to navigate through the pages you have visited.

Note, however, that navigation through Web pages is not tracked for every Web page you visit during a session. Safari uses a sequential navigation method that tracks only the pages along a particular path.

For instance, assume you were browsing Page A, then Pages B, C, and D. On Page D, you found a hyperlink back to Page B and clicked it to visit that page. Now, from Page B again, assume you went off and visited Pages E and F. If you were to use the Back icon in this session, the order of pages that would appear for each click of the Back icon would be F to E to B to A. Pages C and D, because they were on another "track" of browsing, would no longer be a part of the browser's navigation, even if you were to cycle forward through the same pages again using the Forward icon.

One of the nicer features of the iPad is its capability to call up Safari whenever any hyperlink or Web page shortcut is clicked—in any app. That capability is particularly handy when using the Mail app, where you often receive URLs from colleagues.

Another useful feature in Safari is its capability to zoom in on any Web page. There are two ways to go about this while browsing.

The first method is the reverse pinch, or fanning, technique. To zoom in, simply tap the section of the page you want to enlarge and move your fingers apart. The page will zoom in as long as you move your fingers out. Reverse the move to a pinch and zoom back out.

The second method is double-tapping on a particular section of the page. Safari will automatically zoom in to have that section of the page fill the screen. This is particularly useful when visiting a page with a section of useful content surrounded by images and ads. To zoom back to the full-page view, double-tap again.

Managing Bookmarks and History

Human beings are creatures of habit, and often we find ourselves clinging to the familiar as we move through our day. Safari accommodates this trait with its Bookmarks feature. Bookmarks are markers that, when selected in a menu or tapped in the Bookmark toolbar, will take you directly to the Web page you want—without typing the URL address.

You can create a bookmark very easily in Safari. Then, when you need to, you can open up a page with just a couple of taps.

To open a bookmark, tap the Bookmark icon and select the bookmark you want from the action menu (see Figure 6.3). If there is a bookmark within the Bookmark bar, all you need to do is tap it.

Figure 6.3

The Bookmark action menu.

When you find a page you want to save, you can bookmark it and add it to your bookmark collection.

To create a bookmark:

1. From a page you want to save, tap the Add Bookmark icon. The Add Bookmark action menu will open (see Figure 6.4).

2. Tap Add Bookmark. The Add Bookmark pop-over will appear (see Figure 6.5).

3. Confirm or edit the name of the bookmark you want to use.

4. Tap the Bookmarks Bar control if you want the bookmark to appear somewhere other than the main Bookmark menu and then tap a new location.

5. Tap Save. The bookmark will be added to the desired location (see Figure 6.6).

Figure 6.4

The Add Bookmark action menu.

Figure 6.5

The Add Bookmark pop-over.

As time goes on, you may find your collection of bookmarks has grown quite a bit. Safari includes a way to organize bookmarks in a way that makes the best sense for you.

To organize bookmarks:

1. From any page, tap the Bookmark icon. The Bookmark action menu will open.

2. Tap the Edit button. The action menu will shift to Edit mode.

3. Tap and drag the Move icon on any item to move it up or down the list of bookmarks. The Move icon is denoted by three horizontal lines.

4. Tap the New Folder button. The New Folder pop-over will appear.

5. Type a Title for the new folder and tap Bookmarks. The new folder will appear in the Bookmarks action menu.

6. Tap a bookmark's Delete icon; then tap the Delete button. The bookmark will be removed.

7. Tap Done. The menu will reflect the changes you made.

You can also put Bookmarks on any of the home screens. When they appear on a home screen, Bookmarks are referred to as *Web clips*.

To make a Web clip:

1. From a page you want to save, tap the Add Bookmark icon. The Add Bookmark action menu will open.

2. Tap Add to Home Screen. The Add to Home pop-over will appear (see Figure 6.7).

Figure 6.7

The Add to Home pop-over.

3. Edit the name of the Web Clip icon and tap Add. The Web Clip icon will be added to a home screen.

If you've been browsing around a while, and just can't seem to remember that site you visited a couple of days ago (and naturally forgot to bookmark), you can use Safari's history feature to track that site down.

To explore Safari's History feature:

1. From any page, tap the Bookmark icon. The Bookmark action menu will open.

2. Tap the History folder. The History action menu will open (see Figure 6.8).

Figure 6.8

The History action menu.

3. Tap the page you want to revisit. The page will open in Safari.

If you want to clear the history in Safari, the fastest way to accomplish this is through the History action menu.

To clear the History:

1. From any page, tap the Bookmark icon. The Bookmark action menu will open.

2. Tap the History folder. The History action menu will open.

3. Tap the Clear History button. The Safari history will be erased.

Managing Tabbed Browsing

Many PC and Mac-based browsers have a feature known as *tabbed browsing*, which enables the browser to hold multiple pages at once.

Safari on the iPad also features tabs, which is a useful way to handle many pages at the same time.

To work with tabs in Safari:

1. From any page, tap the Add Tab icon (the + at the upper right of the screen). A new Untitled tab will open, as shown in Figure 6.9.

Figure 6.9

A new tab, ready to load.

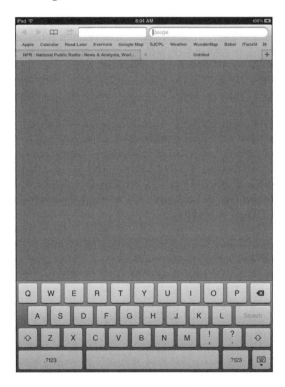

2. Type any URL. The tab will open to that page within Safari.
3. To move a tab, press and drag the tab across the screen to a new location in the tab bar.
4. To close the tab, tap the small close icon on the left side of the tab. The tab will close.

If you tap the Multiple Page icon, you will see the page displayed as one of the minipages. To remove a page, tap the black X icon to remove the page.

Searching for Content

Finding pages on the Web used to be very easy—with only 500 or so websites in existence in the early 90s, you could almost index them by hand. Today, there are billions of Web pages and finding useful information can be daunting sometimes. Safari has a search tool that not only uses the most powerful search tools around, but also allows you to choose the search engines you prefer.

Using the Search bar is easy: Just type in what you are looking for and press Enter. By default, the Search bar connects to the Google search engine, and it will display the results of your search in a new tab.

TIP   Suggestive Searches

Safari will suggest search terms similar to what you type in an effort to save you time. If you see the term you were looking for in the menu, tap it to start the actual search.

To change search engines, you need to use the Settings app:

1. Tap the Settings app icon. The Settings app will open.
2. Tap the Safari setting. The Safari settings pane will open (see Figure 6.10).
3. Tap the Search Engine setting. The Search Engine pane will open.
4. Tap one of the three available options. The selected search engine will be indicated by a check mark.
5. Click the Home button. The new search engine will be used in Safari.

Figure 6.10

The Safari settings.

Customizing Your Browser

Whenever you travel extensively on the Internet, you're bound to run across a few common bumps in the road that could slow you down. Fortunately, Safari has some settings that will smooth out the ride.

One such feature is the AutoFill tool. AutoFill's job is to help you fill in those registration or payment information forms you might run into while surfing the Web. AutoFill uses your own contact information to provide information for those forms when you come across them.

CAUTION   Identity Alert

Using AutoFill is handy, but be aware that if your iPad falls into someone else's hands, Safari could fill in your personal information, including passwords for sensitive websites, like your bank. It's something to keep in mind.

To activate AutoFill:

1. Tap the Settings app icon. The Settings app will open.
2. Tap the Safari setting. The Safari settings pane will open.
3. Tap the AutoFill option. The AutoFill pane will appear.
4. Slide the Use Contact Info control to On. The My Info control will activate.
5. Tap the My Info control. A menu of your contacts will appear.
6. Tap the contact that represents you. That contact will appear in the My Info control.
7. Slide the Names and Passwords control to On. This will keep track of any login names and passwords as you enter them.
8. Click the Home button. The changes will be saved.

If you have surfed the Internet for any length of time, then you know that pop-up windows and ads can be the bane of your Web experience or vital tools. Disreputable sites can use them to force advertising, but legitimate sites also have a use for them. Depending on your Web habits, you may or may not want pop-ups blocked, which is Safari's default setting.

Here's how to turn pop-up blocking off:

1. Tap the Settings app icon. The Settings app will open.
2. Tap the Safari setting. The Safari settings pane will open.
3. Slide the Block Pop-ups control to Off.
4. Click the Home button. The change will be saved.

Cookies are another piece of Web technology that can help or hinder your Web experience. Cookies are little bits of tracking code that websites will "hand" you when you visit. They can enhance your surfing, because when you return to the site, it will "remember" you and your preferences because of the cookie your browser has received from the earlier visit.

The problem is that cookies can represent a security threat because any site can use a cookie to track where you have been on the Web even after you leave the site. Cookies can also be used as delivery mechanisms for some pretty nasty software like viruses. Safari will give you the options not to accept cookies, pick them up just from sites you've visited, or pick them up from any site at all.

Of all of these options, the visited site option is probably the best compromise, but it's a matter of personal preference.

To change the cookie setting:

1. Tap the Settings app icon. The Settings app will open.
2. Tap the Safari setting. The Safari settings pane will open.
3. Tap the Accept Cookies control. The Accept Cookies pane will open.
4. Tap the option you prefer. The selected option will be denoted by a check mark.
5. Click the Home button. The change will be saved.

Conclusion

In this chapter, you learned some of the finer points of operating the Safari browser, a flexible and fast window to the Internet.

In Chapter 7, "Communicating with Email," we will examine how to use the other most-used aspect of the Internet: email, and how the iPad's Mail app handles this important job.

Chapter 7
Communicating with Email

It is not entirely clear when the use of email began to be so indispensible, but it was a fast adoption. When the Internet was opened to the general public in the mid 1990s, businesses were relatively quick to adopt email. The prospect of being able to send messages of virtually any length instantaneously to anyone in the world with an email address was simply too great a communications tool to ignore. As time went on, the general public embraced email, too, making it a very popular way to keep in touch.

The iPad is endowed with a built-in email app, cleverly named *Mail*. Don't let the simple name fool you—this is a robust and versatile application.

If you've used any email application on a PC or Mac, there's a lot about Mail that you are going to recognize, so let's get started.

In this chapter, you will learn how to do the following:

* Create an email account
* Download your messages
* Organize your email

Setting Up an Account

Getting an email account these days is a pretty simple thing. Most Internet service providers often provide multiple email accounts per Internet connection—one for each member of the family. They are also often free to use, and have storage limits that are usually too big for the average person to concern themselves with.

Whenever you set up a new email account, your Internet service provider will provide you with some important information that you need to memorize or store in a safe place somewhere.

For an email account from an Internet provider, you will need:

* Your new email address
* Your user name for the POP or IMAP server
* Your password for the POP or IMAP server
* The Internet address of the POP or IMAP server

Don't worry about what the POP and IMAP servers are—these are just technical names for the types of machines that handle your incoming and outgoing email messages. But you will need the connection information to fill into the right place in the Mail app.

For other accounts, such as iCloud or Gmail, Mail only needs your username and password. Gmail is especially interesting, because Google provides such accounts to anyone, free of charge, which makes them very useful and easy to set up.

When you first start Mail, you will immediately be given the opportunity to set up an email account. You can set up as many accounts as you would like, but you should have the complete set of information for at least one of your accounts ready to go when you start Mail for the first time. Here's how to set up an account on Gmail, the aforementioned email service from Google:

To set up an account on Gmail:

1. Tap the Mail app icon. The Welcome to Mail screen will open (see Figure 7.1).
2. Tap the Gmail option. The Gmail form will open (see Figure 7.2).
3. Type the appropriate information in the fields. It is important that you fill out all the fields.
4. Tap Save. After verification, the Mail app will open, download your messages, and display the latest message (see Figure 7.3).

Figure 7.1
*Welcome to
Mail.*

Figure 7.2
*Provide your
Gmail
account info.*

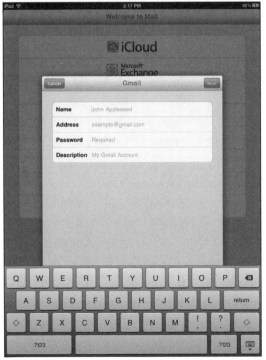

Figure 7.3

Your email, displayed.

If have an account from your Internet service provider, you will use the POP or IMAP server information they should provide to get your account set up.

To use your POP or IMAP server information to set up your account:

1. Tap the Mail app icon. The Welcome to Mail screen will open.

2. Tap the Other option. The New Account form will open.

3. Type the appropriate information in the fields. It is important that you fill out all the fields.

4. Tap Save. Mail will determine if your mail server uses IMAP or POP. When it does, the Enter your account information form will open, as shown in Figure 7.4.

5. Tap the POP or IMAP button, depending on the type of account you have.

6. Type your account information into the appropriate fields.

7. Click Save. After verification, the Mail app will open, download your messages, and display the latest message.

Figure 7.4

*Provide your
POP or
IMAP
account info.*

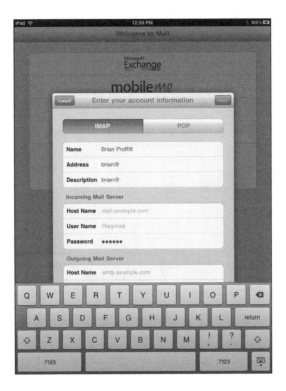

Your account is set to manually download email by default, which means email will be downloaded only when you specify or when you first start Mail.

To set Mail to download email automatically:

1. Tap the Settings app icon. The Settings screen will open.
2. Tap the Mail, Contacts, Calendars setting. The Mail, Contacts, Calendars setting pane will open (see Figure 7.5).
3. Tap the Fetch New Data setting. The Fetch New Data pane will open (see Figure 7.6).
4. Tap the interval option you want. The selected option will be denoted by a check mark.
5. Click the Home button. The options will be saved.

Figure 7.5

The Mail, Contacts, Calendars setting pane.

Figure 7.6

Configure how often you want to get email.

TIP **Taking It Easy on the Email Server**

You can set Mail to download email automatically at a certain interval. The fastest interval is 15 minutes, so you don't overload your POP server. That's a good idea if you're connecting through 3G or 4G. If you can manage the timing of email downloads, you can control the flow of traffic through your wireless connection.

If you want to add another email account to Mail, you will need to use the Welcome to Mail tool again.

To access the Welcome to Mail tool, follow these steps in the Settings app:

1. Tap the Settings app icon. The Settings screen will open.

2. Tap the Mail, Contacts, Calendars setting. The Mail, Contacts, Calendars setting pane will open.

3. Tap the Add Account setting. The Add Account pane will open (see Figure 7.7).

Figure 7.7

Adding an additional account.

4. Tap the type of account you want to add and follow the steps you used in the Welcome to Mail screen to complete the task.

Receiving and Sending Email

Once you have one account set up in Mail, you are free to send and receive email as long as you are connected to the Internet.

> **NOTE** **Checking for New Email**
>
> If you did not set Mail to download messages automatically (or just want to see what's out there before the next scheduled download occurs), tap the Inbox button and then the Reload icon at the bottom of the Inbox menu. Your messages will be downloaded.

As you can see in Figure 7.8, the Mail app is very simple.

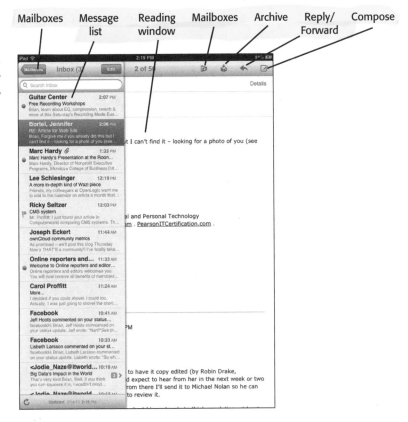

Figure 7.8

The vertical Mail interface.

Reading a message is simple: Just tap the Inbox folder; then tap a message in the Message list, and its contents will be displayed in the Reading window.

After you have read an email, you will note that the blue dot icon next to the message in the Message list will be removed.

If you want to always see the Message list, turn the iPad 90 degrees until the Mail app is displayed horizontally (see Figure 7.9). You can tap messages in the Message pane and read them in the Reading pane.

Figure 7.9

The horizontal Mail interface.

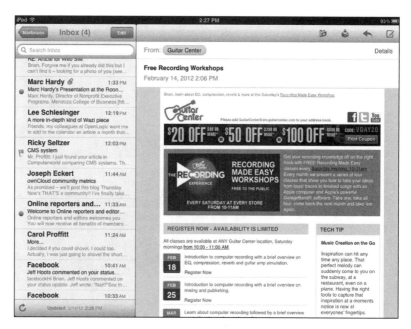

Of course, you can do more with an email than just read it. In fact, more often than not, a message will warrant a reply.

To reply to the *sender* of the message only:

1. Open a message to which you want to reply. The message will be displayed in the Reading window.

2. Tap the Reply/Forward icon. The Reply/Forward action menu will open.

One Reply or Many?

Mail is clever enough to notice when you have received an email sent to just you or to other people, too. If the message has multiple recipients, the Reply to All option will be visible on the Reply/Forward action menu.

3. Tap Reply. A preaddressed Compose window will open (see Figure 7.10).

Figure 7.10

Replying to a message.

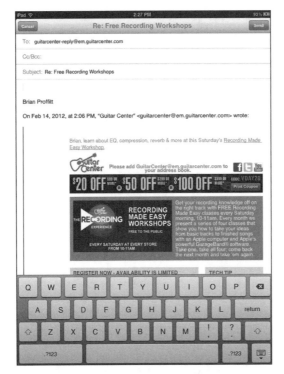

4. Type your reply in the body of the message.

5. When finished, tap Send. The Message window will close, and with a whoosh sound effect, the message will be sent.

If the message was sent to you and other people, you can send a reply to all the recipients and the sender.

To send a reply to all the recipients and the sender:

1. Tap a message to reply to all recipients. The message will be displayed in the Reading window.
2. Tap the Reply/Forward icon. The Reply/Forward action menu will open.
3. Tap Reply to All. A preaddressed Compose window will open.
4. Type your reply in the body of the message.
5. When finished, tap Send. The Message window will close, and with a whoosh sound effect, the message will be sent.

To forward a message to someone else:

1. Tap a message to forward. The message will be displayed in the Reading window.
2. Tap the Reply/Forward icon. The Reply/Forward action menu will open.
3. Tap Forward. A preaddressed Compose window will open.
4. Type an additional message in the body of the message.
5. When finished, tap Send. The Message window will close, and with a whoosh sound effect, the message will be sent.

To send a new message to a single or multiple recipients:

1. Tap the Compose icon. A Compose Message window will open (see Figure 7.11).
2. Type an email address in the To field.

NOTE   Contact Connection

If you use the Contacts tool on the iPad, tap the blue + icon on the right end of the To:, Cc:, or Bcc: fields to open the All Contacts list. Tap the addresses you need without typing a single ampersand.

3. If you need to blind carbon copy a recipient, tap the Cc/Bcc: field to open separate Cc: and Bcc: fields and type the address in.
4. Type a Subject.

Figure 7.11

A new Message window.

5. Type a message in the body.

6. Tap Send. The Message window will close, and with a whoosh sound effect, the message will be sent.

Organizing Mail

After you have read your messages and sent your replies, what next? You don't want to leave your Inbox cluttered, and unless it's junk mail, you don't want to delete everything, either.

Mail is very good about handling lots of email at once. Let's take some steps to organize the Inbox first.

If you tap the Inbox button and then tap the Mailboxes control, you will see a list of mailboxes with which to filter the Message list (see Figure 7.12). Usually, these mailboxes are folders or categories imported from your email account. Tap these mailboxes, as desired, to see the results on your Message list.

Figure 7.12

Viewing your mailboxes.

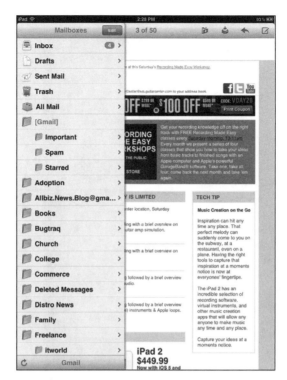

The mailbox is a really useful tool in Mail for organizing your information. Using mailboxes, you can essentially treat messages as files, which is what they are. Mail cannot create or change mailboxes—this has to be done directly within your account.

To move messages into folders:

1. Tap a message to organize. The message will be displayed in the Reading window.

2. Tap the Mailboxes icon. The Mailboxes list will open (see Figure 7.13).

3. Tap the mailbox into which you want to move the message. The message will "fly" into the mailbox, and the latest message in your Inbox will be displayed.

To move a number of messages into a folder:

1. Tap the Inbox button. The Message list will open.

2. Tap the Edit button. The list will shift into Edit mode (see Figure 7.14).

Figure 7.13
Organizing with mailboxes.

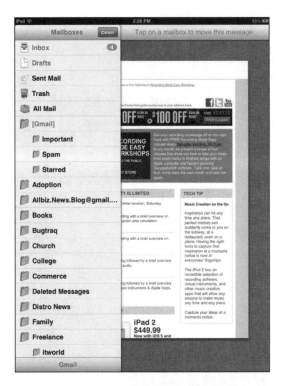

Figure 7.14
Editing the Inbox.

3. Tap the messages you want to move into a mailbox. The messages will be selected by red check mark icons and "stacked" in the Reading window (see Figure 7.15).

Figure 7.15

Selecting multiple messages.

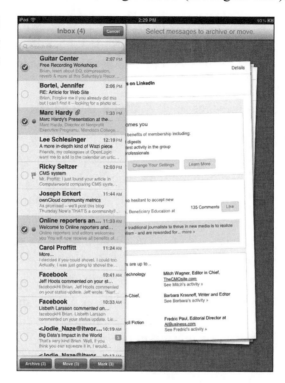

4. Tap the Move button. The Mailboxes list will open.

5. Tap the mailbox into which you want to move the messages. The messages will "fly" into the mailbox, and the latest message in your Inbox will be displayed.

To delete individual messages:

1. Tap a message to delete. The message will be displayed in the Reading window.

2. Tap the Delete icon. The message will be deleted.

To delete multiple messages (just like organizing multiple emails):

1. Tap the Inbox button. The Message list will open.

2. Tap the Edit button. The list will shift into Edit mode.

3. Tap the messages you want to delete. The messages will be selected by red check mark icons and "stacked" in the Reading window.

4. Tap the Delete button. The messages will be deleted.

If, perchance, you happened to delete a message that shouldn't have been trashed, don't panic because you can still get the message back.

To get a message back that you've deleted:

1. Tap the Inbox button. The Message list will open.

2. Tap the Mailboxes button. The Mailboxes list will open.

3. Tap the Trash mailbox. The Trash list will appear.

4. Tap the Edit button. The Trash list will shift into Edit mode.

5. Tap the messages you want to recover. The messages will be selected by red check mark icons and "stacked" in the Reading window.

6. Tap the Move button. The Mailboxes list will open.

7. Tap the mailbox into which you want to move the messages. The messages will "fly" into the mailbox, and the latest message in your Inbox will be displayed.

Conclusion

There is a lot more to email these days than just reading and writing: It's a way to keep in touch with family and friends all around the world. With this medium becoming so integrated in our daily lives, it's good to see that there are excellent tools in the iPad that can make email use easy.

In Chapter 8, "Video Calls with FaceTime," you will discover an app that will let you see your friends and family face-to-face with Internet video calling.

Chapter 8
Video Calls with FaceTime

In the 21st century, we were all supposed to have flying cars. And instant-cook kitchens. And video phone calls. So far, it hasn't been a great century for futurists who based their ideas on episodes of *The Jetsons*.

But the new century hasn't been a complete bust for technology that once seemed too fantastical to believe: Videoconferencing has become a not-so-rare fixture for boardrooms and high-end school technology centers. This technology, which uses the ubiquitous Internet to connect dedicated videoconferencing devices to one another, is a definite step toward the future.

And there is a cost, usually a literal one: Such devices are costly and typically out of the reach of most schools and certainly out of reach for most parents.

Webcams have been a fair substitute, but they are also usually tied down to stationary machines and as such are not very portable. They are also typically not high-quality devices, with configuration sometimes being a challenge.

One of the more innovative features available for the iPad is Apple's FaceTime app, which finally delivers on the promise of affordable, portable, and decent quality videoconferencing to individual users. In this chapter, you will learn how to:

❋ Set up FaceTime

❋ Connect to FaceTime users you know

❋ Make a FaceTime call

What Is FaceTime?

FaceTime is not something new to the iPad, although the iPad 2 was the first model that could actually use it, thanks to the on-board front- and rear-facing cameras. FaceTime was actually created for the iPhone 4 in the summer of 2010, the first device from Apple to feature a dual-camera setup.

It's this double-camera configuration that makes FaceTime work so well on the iPad 2 and 2012 iPad. Until recently, most mobile devices, when they had a camera, used a photo/video capture lens that was located on the back of the device—in other words, the side of the device that was on the opposite side of the device's video screen. Think about a two-way video call and you can quickly imagine such a situation becoming very awkward, very quickly.

FaceTime can enable you and your friends and family to easily engage in video calls with any FaceTime-enabled device in the world.

But in that statement alone, there are hidden limitations. Note that connectivity is limited to other FaceTime-equipped devices. Right now, that includes all iPad 2 and 2012 iPad devices, any iPhone 4 (and newer), fourth-generation iPod Touch devices (and newer), and any desktop or laptop with Mac OS X 10.6.6 or higher. So we're not exactly talking about a small user base.

Still, as of press time, Windows users were not able to use FaceTime, and don't look for FaceTime on the Android smartphones anytime soon, either, given the animosity between Apple and Google over their respective mobile platforms.

This means that as you seek out possible connections for FaceTime, you will need to deliberately search for friends and family who have the correct devices.

Another, perhaps more well-known limitation is the inability for FaceTime devices to send their signals over any cellular network. This is due to the sheer amount of data each video call creates—far too much for any cellular plan to easily and cheaply handle. Using FaceTime for a call of any significant length over cellular 3G or 4G service could be a very expensive proposition.

What all of this means is that anyone using FaceTime on the iPad must connect over a wireless network. This WiFi-only limitation still gets quite a bit of knocking in the media, but to be honest, most iPad owners can usually find a wireless network somewhere.

The good news is, once you find such a network, it is very simple to set up a FaceTime connection. But first, you need to configure FaceTime to be ready to receive and send calls.

Setting Up FaceTime

When you first use your iPad, FaceTime will likely be disabled by default. That's because you must register your contact information with the FaceTime app so that callers can reach you. This contact information is in the form of an email address, one of which must be added to FaceTime.

To register your FaceTime-equipped iPad:

1. Tap the Settings icon on the home screen. The Settings app will open.

2. Tap the FaceTime setting. The FaceTime sign-in pane will open, as seen in Figure 8.1.

3. Type the email address or user name for your Apple ID into the user name field.

4. Type your Apple ID password into the password field.

5. Tap the Sign In button. The address confirmation screen will appear (see Figure 8.2).

6. Tap the Next button. The address will be accepted, and the FaceTime settings pane will appear (see Figure 8.3).

Figure 8.1

The FaceTime sign-in pane.

Figure 8.2

Confirm the address you want to use for FaceTime.

Figure 8.3

The FaceTime settings pane.

If you ever decide to disable your FaceTime app, you can use the Settings app to manage this.

To disable FaceTime:

1. Tap the Settings icon on the home screen. The Settings app will open.

2. Tap the FaceTime setting. The FaceTime settings pane will open.

3. Slide the FaceTime control to Off. FaceTime will be disabled on your iPad.

Once FaceTime is initially configured, you can give the email address you entered to friends and family to use to contact you with their FaceTime devices.

Making a FaceTime Call

Very likely the hardest part of making a FaceTime call is finding someone with whom to connect. If your circle of friends and colleagues are dedicated Apple users, this problem is a bit easier to manage.

To date, there is no app or online directory that enables you to find out which of your contacts has FaceTime capabilities. You will need to find them using the old-fashioned way: Ask them.

Once you identify someone with whom you or your student can connect, the rest is a breeze.

Here's how to make a FaceTime call:

1. Tap the FaceTime app icon. The FaceTime home screen will appear (see Figure 8.4).

Figure 8.4

The FaceTime home screen.

2. Tap a contact with whom you want to connect. The call will start immediately.

3. When the recipient answers, her image will appear in the large screen and your image will appear in the smaller picture-in-picture, as shown in Figure 8.5.

Figure 8.5

A call in progress.

4. When the call is complete, tap the End Call button. The call will end, and the home screen will appear.

That's pretty much it; nothing fancy is needed. The quality settings are all automatic, though it's always good to have plenty of light available when making any video call.

When a call comes into FaceTime, a trilling tone will sound, and you will be given the choice to Accept or Decline the incoming call. Tap Accept, and the call will begin, as shown in Figure 8.6.

Another feature of FaceTime makes use of the rear-facing camera, so you can show the caller something else while still being able to view them on the iPad screen. For instance, a student who wants to share an art project could use the rear camera to show off his work, while still watching his caller on-screen.

Figure 8.6

An incoming call.

To use this feature, simply tap the camera switch button during a call. To reactivate the front-facing camera, tap the camera switch button again.

Conclusion

In this chapter, you learned about a really nice iPad feature to connect to family and friends, FaceTime, and how easy it is to set up and use to contact any other FaceTime user.

The FaceTime app is a great way for you to interact with friends and family, and even communicate with acquaintances anywhere in the world.

The iPad is about more than just communication. It's also about learning. And what better way to learn than reading a book? In Chapter 9, "iBooks for Reading," you will discover just how to find, buy, and read literary works in just moments.

Chapter 9
iBooks for Reading

Since the invention of the personal computer, industry observers have constantly predicted the death of books.

The written works of humankind, they argue, would no longer be found in the bound-paper format that collects dust on the bookshelves of the world, but rather in the form of electrons displaying information on a screen.

And yet it hasn't come to pass. Books, newspapers, and magazines are still printed by the millions, with only small signs of slowing down.

But consumer acceptance of electronic books is slowly changing. When Amazon.com introduced the Kindle portable reading device in 2007, it was selling a device with easy-to-read text and a delivery method superior to any other device at the time—free cellular data access. This meant that you could buy a book anywhere with cell coverage and have it delivered to you for just the cost of the book—and no shipping.

The iPad's form factor makes it an ideal device for reading electronic books, too. Although access to buying books is limited to WiFi or a paid 3G or 4G plan, it's still very easy to get a copy of the latest bestselling novel, book to read to your grandkids, or magazine on the iPad in seconds.

In this chapter, learn how to use the iBooks app to:

* Find electronic books in the iBooks Store
* Purchase books for the iPad
* Read your purchased books

Finding Your Reading Material

iBooks is the free app from Apple that, while not included with the iPad, is strongly suggested as your first downloaded app when you first connect to the iTunes Store with the iPad. If you didn't download it then, you should go ahead and download it to start your iPad reading experience.

To buy a book for iBooks:

1. Tap the iBooks icon to start the iBooks app. The first time it starts, you will be asked to sync your reading progress and bookmarks (see Figure 9.1).

Figure 9.1

Syncing iBooks.

2. Tap the Sync option you want. The primary iBooks screen (an empty bookshelf) will appear.

3. Tap the Store button. The Store screen will appear (see Figure 9.2).

TIP — **Syncing Explained**

As you read your books, iBooks will keep track of your progress, as well as any bookmarks you might have inserted in your books. If you plan to read your book on another iBooks-equipped device, such as an iPhone, synchronization will enable the other device to pick up right where you left off on the iPad and copy your bookmarks. If you don't have other iBooks devices, tap Don't Sync.

Figure 9.2

*The iBooks
Store.*

4. Tap the Search button bar and type the title or author name you're looking for. Suggested options will be displayed in the Suggestions menu as you type.

5. Tap the book or author name that matches your search. The results will be displayed on the Search screen, as shown in Figure 9.3.

6. Tap the book you want to view. The book's page will open (see Figure 9.4).

7. To read more about the book, tap the More link below the Description paragraph.

8. To find out how other users liked the book, read the Customer Reviews section.

9. When satisfied you want to buy this book, tap the price button at the top of the window. The button will change to a green Buy Book button.

10. Tap the Buy Book button. A login dialog box will appear.

Figure 9.3

*Finding the
book you
want.*

Figure 9.4

*The book's
information
page.*

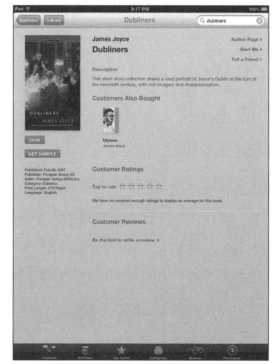

11. Enter your iTunes Password information for the iTunes Store and tap OK. The book will be downloaded, with the progress shown on the main iBooks screen (see Figure 9.5).

Figure 9.5

Downloading a book.

NOTE   **Redeem Your Gift Cards**

If you have an iTunes Gift Card or Gift Certificate, tap the Redeem button on the bottom of most pages in the iBooks Store and then provide your gift card information. If you purchase books, you will be given the choice to use the redeemed gift card amount or the payment method associated with your iTunes account, which is used by iBooks.

Reading in iBooks

After you have a book downloaded, reading it is simply a matter of tapping the book on the iBooks shelf to open it (see Figure 9.6).

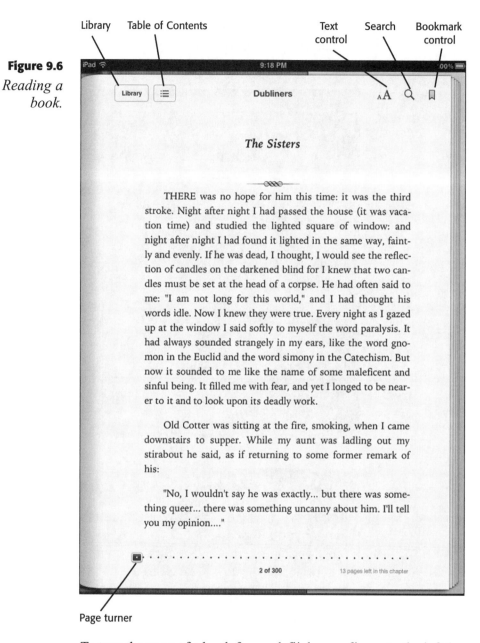

Figure 9.6

Reading a book.

To turn the page of a book forward, flick your finger to the left (as if you were flipping a paper page). You can also tap the right edge of the page.

To flip back a page, flick your finger to the right or tap the left edge of the page.

Navigating beyond one page at a time can be done a couple of ways. Tap anywhere on the page to bring up the page controls seen in Figure 9.6. Then tap the Table of Contents button to view the Table of Contents page.

To move to another location in the book, tap any of the chapter or section headers that are visible. The book will be opened to that spot.

If you have any bookmarks inserted in the book, you can use the Bookmarks page to navigate to that bookmark. Tap the Table of Contents button and in the Table of Contents page, tap the Bookmarks button. Any bookmarks in the book will be listed, as shown in Figure 9.7. Tap the bookmark to view that page.

Figure 9.7

The Bookmarks page.

You can also use the page-turner control found on the bottom of every page when you tap the page. Tap and drag the rectangular control to move to the page number you want. When you lift your finger, the desired page will open.

You can use the Brightness and Text controls to adjust the text size and display properties of the iBooks app.

If this seems simple, that's because it's designed to be that way. iBooks is meant to be simple, so you can do the thing you really need to do—read.

Conclusion

Reading a good book can be a great source of satisfaction. But sometimes you are in the mood for something a little more entertaining.

The iPad can be a great source of entertainment to use for trips or just for a lazy day. In Chapter 10, "Entertainment with iTunes," we'll take a look at one of the most central iPad apps, iTunes, and find out how to listen to music and watch movies to your heart's content.

Chapter 10
Entertainment with iTunes

In Chapter 1, "First Step: Introducing the iPad," you learned about the origins of the iPad and its relationship with earlier Apple devices, such as the iPod, iPhone, and iPod Touch.

When it first appeared, the iPad was derisively referred to as a giant iPod Touch, and in some ways that description had some truth to it. The interfaces were similar, and there was quite a bit of shared functionality. If that's the case, then like the iPod Touch, the iPad should be able to display multimedia files with relative ease.

And that is indeed within the iPad's capabilities. Since the screen is much larger than its iPod and iPhone cousins, the iPad does a superior job of showing the latest movies and television shows with the Videos app. It is also a great music player, thanks to the Music app.

In this chapter, you'll learn how to:

* Purchase multimedia content in the iTunes store
* Acquire an audio podcast
* Play back multimedia content on the iPad
* Find and view YouTube content

Getting Multimedia: iTunes

As you learned in Chapter 4, "Fourth Step: Using the iPad Apps," the content of iTunes on your desktop machine is identical to its iPad counterpart in terms of apps. This is also the case with music and movies in the iTunes store.

Finding and installing multimedia content with the iPad is just as easy as using the iTunes application. To get an idea of how you can purchase content for the iPad, here's how to find and purchase a music album with the iTunes app.

To find and purchase music using iTunes:

1. Tap the iTunes icon to start the iTunes app (see Figure 10.1).

Figure 10.1

The iTunes app.

2. Tap the Music button on the iTunes toolbar if it's not on the Music page already.

3. Tap the Search bar and type in the artist or album name you're looking for. Suggested options will be displayed in the Suggestions menu as you type.

4. Tap the artist or album name that matches your search. The results will be displayed on the Search screen, as shown in Figure 10.2.

Figure 10.2

Tracking down music.

5. Tap the album or song you want to view. The album's pop-over window will open (see Figure 10.3).

6. To find out how other users liked the music, read the Customer Reviews section.

7. When satisfied you want to buy this album, tap the price button at the top of the window. The button will change to a green Buy Album button.

8. Tap the Buy Album button. A login dialog box will appear.

9. Enter your iTunes Password information for the iTunes Store and tap OK. The album will be downloaded, as shown on the Downloads page (see Figure 10.4).

Figure 10.3

The album's window.

Figure 10.4

Downloading music.

TIP **Redeem Your Gift Cards**

If you have an iTunes Gift Card or Gift Certificate, tap the Redeem button on the bottom of most pages in the iTunes Store and then provide your gift card information. If you purchase music or videos, you will be given the choice to use the redeemed gift card amount or the payment method associated with your iTunes account.

The procedure for buying video content, be it movies or TV shows, is identical to acquiring music. With music, you can buy whole albums or individual songs (although getting the whole album is typically less expensive per song). If you buy TV shows, you can get one episode at a time or an entire season's worth of content.

Getting audio books also uses a similar process, although usually you can only buy the entire book. Many audio books have a Preview feature that allows you to hear some of the content before you purchase it.

Multimedia Playback: Music and Videos

One major difference between the iPad version of iTunes and the desktop version is that the desktop version allows you to play back videos and music right from within the iTunes application.

On the iPad, this functionality is not within the iTunes app, but instead is handled by other specialized apps. Any audio files (music, audio podcasts, and audio books) can be listened to via the Music app, and video content (movies, TV shows, and video podcasts) can be viewed by the Videos app.

To listen to audio content in the Music app:

1. Tap the Music app icon. The Music app will open as seen in Figure 10.5.
2. To view the music content by album, tap the Albums button. The Albums page will appear, as seen in Figure 10.6.

Figure 10.5

The Music app.

Figure 10.6

The Albums page.

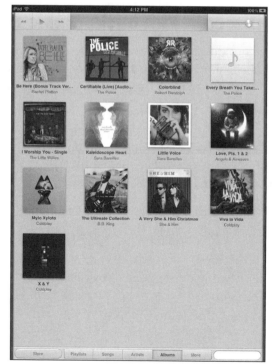

3. Tap the album to play. The album's pop-over window will appear.

4. Tap any song in the album. The album will begin to play from that point.

5. To stop or otherwise control the playback, tap the album cover. The playback controls will appear, enabling you to fast forward, reverse, control volume, and so on.

6. To return to the Music screen, tap any part of the screen other than the raised album cover.

Listening to an audio book or podcast is similar, although these categories are not as organized as the Music section of the iPod Library, since typically you will have a lot more songs to organize than podcasts and audio books. Simply find the book or podcast to listen to and tap it to start playback.

To watch videos:

1. Tap the Videos app icon. Videos will open, as seen in Figure 10.7.

Figure 10.7
The Videos app.

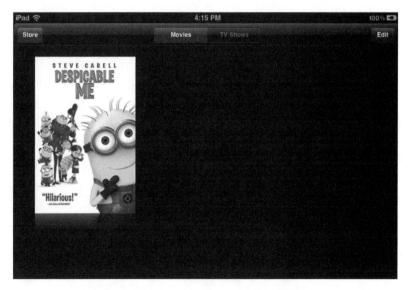

2. To view a TV episode, tap the TV Shows button. The TV Shows page will appear.

3. Tap the video to play. The video's playback information screen will appear (see Figure 10.8).

Figure 10.8

The video's playback information screen.

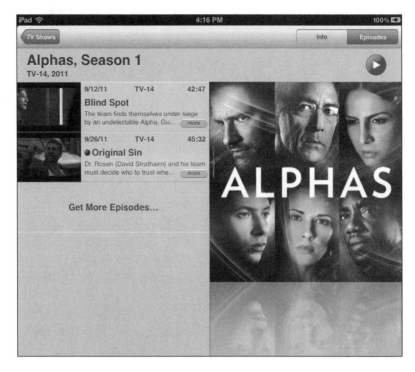

4. Tap the episode to watch and then the Play control. The video will begin to play.

5. To stop or otherwise control the playback, tap the video. The playback controls will appear, enabling you to fast forward, reverse, control volume, and so on.

6. To return to the playback information screen, tap the Done button.

7. To return to the main Videos screen, tap the TV Shows button.

Conclusion

As video and audio content become easier for businesses to create, having a mobile platform to view or listen to such content is a big advantage. The iPad will connect you to a myriad of useful content, as well as more entertaining content to keep you relaxed while on the road.

In Chapter 11, "Sharing Memories," you'll find out how the iPad performs as a still and video camera, so you can capture your friends, family, and special events in digital memory.

Chapter 11
Sharing Memories

The iPad is a surprisingly good platform for recording videos and photos. Because of it's size, it's likely not the best photography device in the world, but it will more than do in a pinch. The iPad 2 and 2012 iPad, in particular, are both suitable for this kind of work, thanks to their onboard video and still camera. With this feature, you can capture images and edit them directly within the iPad.

This chapter will focus on apps from Apple designed specifically for the photos and videos. Specifically, you will explore:

* Camera, an app included with the iPad that turns the device into a simple point-and-shoot camera
* Photo Booth, another iPad app that generates nifty special effects on the fly
* iMovie, an Apple app available for purchase that enables users to record and edit movies taken on any iOS device with a camera onboard

Shutterbugging 101

Cameras used to be a thing that you would have to lug along with you on family trips, for your parents to grab candid shots of you with ice cream on your nose at the beach, or running away from the bear that entered your campground. Or, more likely, making you stand next to your cousins in an unnatural pose (standing still) to get a picture of everyone for the annual family reunion picture, or taking pictures of you waiting at the top of the stairs to see what gifts Saint Nicholas had delivered overnight.

Cameras used to be formal devices, to be treated reverently. Photos would be taken, but then you would not see them until you had taken the film into the photo-processing center for developing. It would sometimes be days before you saw the final product… only to find that while every cousin in the family looked angelic, you were crossing your eyes at the camera.

Today, cameras are digital, and you can see what you have taken instantly. They are also pretty much everywhere—it is hard to find a cell phone these days that *doesn't* have a camera onboard. This ubiquity has led to some startling changes in the photo industry. Film-processing centers are gone, replaced by photo-printing services, which basically use giant printers designed to print images on photo paper or outsource them to specialized printing services to get the same images on T-shirts, coffee mugs, and calendars.

What's nice about having a camera on the iPad is that it gives you an opportunity to snap off a quick picture from the same device that you are playing or working with. This is called convergence—where fewer devices start performing a multitude of tasks. Like Swiss Army knives.

There are some drawbacks to the cameras on the iPad that should be mentioned up front: there is no flash device on the iPad, so any pictures you take must be in natural light. The capabilities of the camera itself are good, although not stunning. The camera resolution is only 720 pixels on the iPad 2 and 5 megapixels on the 2012 iPad. Don't expect high-quality images from the iPad 2 camera and make sure that you have a lot of light even for the 2012 iPad.

This is not meant to discourage you from using the iPad for capturing images, but it is important to set realistic expectations for what the camera can do. If you need quick images that are snapped spontaneously, the iPad is more than appropriate for the job.

As you may have noticed throughout the book, the camera's functionality can be embedded within other apps you may be using. Typically, you can use it to snap a picture of yourself that can be used as a personal icon in the app you are using.

To take a photo with either of the two cameras on the iPad, tap the Camera app icon to start the camera. The image from the rear-facing camera will appear, as shown in Figure 11.1.

Figure 11.1

*The Camera
app in action.*

Last picture taken   Options   Take picture   Switch cameras   Still/video switch

The Camera app is very simple: Point the iPad at the person or thing you want to photograph; then tap the Camera icon in the right center of the screen. A shutter animation and sound effect will indicate the picture has been taken.

If you want to use the front-facing camera and take a picture of the person actually holding the iPad, then tap the switch camera button to activate that camera. Tap the Take picture button to snap the picture as you normally would (see Figure 11.2).

Figure 11.2

The author in action.

Pictures taken with the camera are stored in the standard camera roll storage area on the iPad. Tap the Last picture taken control in the lower-left corner of the Camera screen to open the Photos app to view that picture and any others you may have taken (see Figure 11.3).

You can view photos by swiping back and forth between photos or tapping the appropriate image along the image navigation bar along the bottom of the screen.

The Camera app is not the only iPad app that grabs images. Photo Booth is a fun little app that's also included with the tablet that simulates some cool effects with which kids will love to play.

Tap the Photo Booth app icon, and you will see a screen like the one shown in Figure 11.4, with nine different views of what the camera is picking up at the moment.

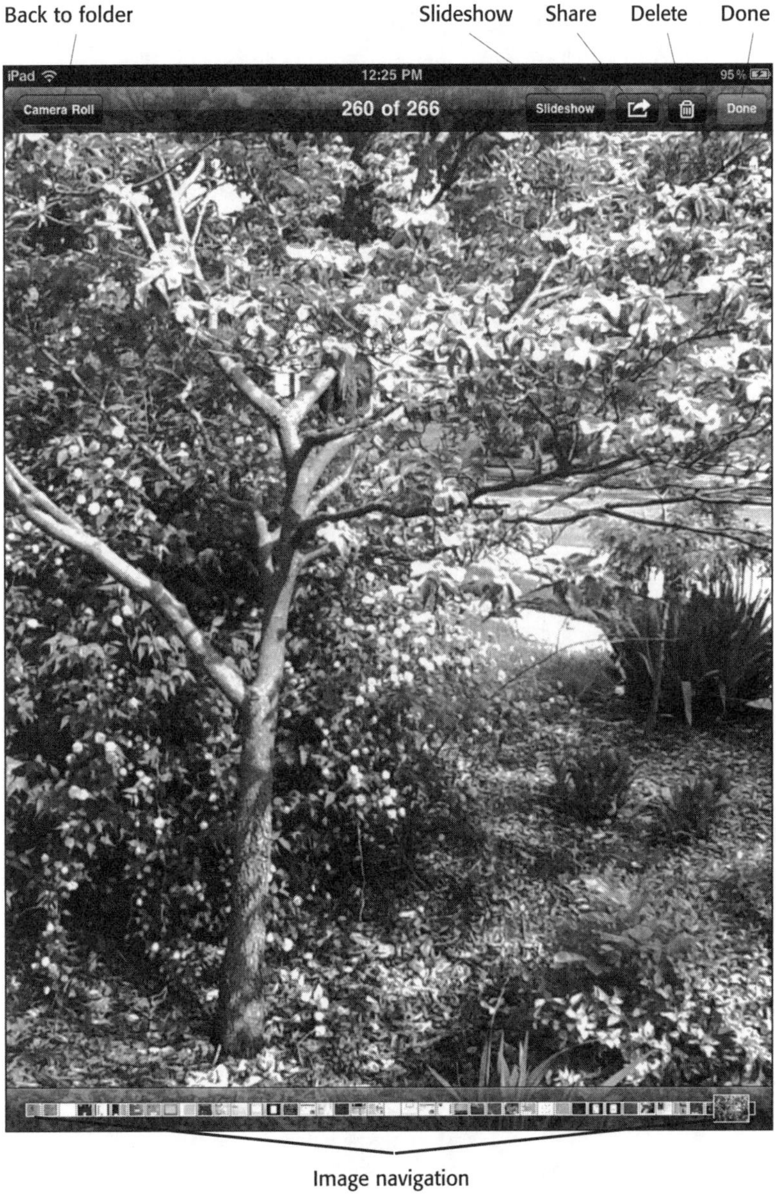
Back to folder
Slideshow
Share
Delete
Done
iPad
12:25 PM
95%
Camera Roll
260 of 266
Slideshow
Done
Image navigation

Figure 11.3
Viewing a photo in Photos.

Figure 11.4

The Photo Booth views.

Beyond the Normal view in the center of this screen, there are eight other views presented within Photo Booth. The effects are self-explanatory and visually very interesting. Move the camera around to find the visual effect that's most pleasing to you. When you see something you want to take a photo of, tap the effect window you desire. The window will expand to fill the iPad 2 screen so you can frame the photo, as seen in Figure 11.5.

Once you have the image framed with the desired effect, tap the picture icon to snap the shot.

NOTE **Special Effects Only**

The Thermal Camera and X-Ray image effects are just that: effects. The Thermal Camera image is just a false-color image based on the amount of light and color of the object being tracked, not an actual infrared camera. The X-Ray effect is basically a negative version of the black-and-white image from the camera. You can't actually see through things.

Figure 11.5

Taking a "thermal" picture.

Last photos taken with Photo Booth

Effects window   Take picture   Switch cameras

Quiet on Set!

Like digital cameras, it's not too hard to find video cameras in devices these days. Higher-end phones have video capabilities, and point-and-shoot devices are on the market now for less than $200.

The iPad 2's cameras also have video capabilities, enabling you to capture video quickly and easily. You can record videos using the Camera app, by swiping the Still/video switch and then tapping the Record button. When recording, a timer will appear in the upper-right corner of the screen to display the current duration of the video shot. To stop recording, tap the flashing Record button.

NOTE **Framing the Shot**

You can record a video with the iPad 2 in the vertical position, but it could be difficult to frame the shot properly. If you view the video on another device, chances are that device will be more horizontally oriented, so your iPad 2 should be, too.

To view a video taken with the Camera app, tap the Last picture/video taken button to open the Photos app and navigate to the video, as shown in Figure 11.6.

Back to folder   Play/Pause button   Timeline   Share   Delete   Done

Figure 11.6

Viewing a video in Photos.

Image navigation

Tap the video image to start the video playback. To stop the playback, tap the Pause button in the top of the screen.

Using the Camera app to take video will get you straightforward video clips that you can quickly show to others in their raw, unedited form. If you want to create more sophisticated movies with music and effects, you can use the iMovie app from Apple to put together some nice content from your iPad 2.

TIP   **Device Content Only**

One of the big limitations of iMovie is its inability to use video within the app that is recorded from other sources. While you can import still images and music onto the iPad using the usual methods, video recorded on non-iOS cameras can't be used. Only video from iPod Touch and iPhone devices with video camera (or another iPad) can be used.

When iMovie is first started, it will display a message box asking to use your current location. Tap OK if this is acceptable, and the iMovie My Projects screen will appear (see Figure 11.7).

iMovie, like most video-editing applications, handles video content as projects. All of the video, image, and audio clips used in creating a movie are contained within a single project. This is important to keep in mind as you put a video together. In the initial home screen in Figure 11.7, you are invited to start a new project by tapping the + icon. Tap the New Project icon to open the project-editing screen shown in Figure 11.8.

You can use video recorded from the Camera app or record video from within the iMovie app. Tap the Record video button to start recording, as seen in Figure 11.9.

When you are done recording, tap the flashing Record button to stop the video camera and display the Clip Review screen, as shown in Figure 11.10.

Project information marquee

Figure 11.7

*The iMovie
My Projects
screen.*

Download
project
from
iTunes

Help   Add new project   Playback   Share   Delete

Video clips   Playback monitor   Play button   Record audio

Figure 11.8
*Starting a
new project.*

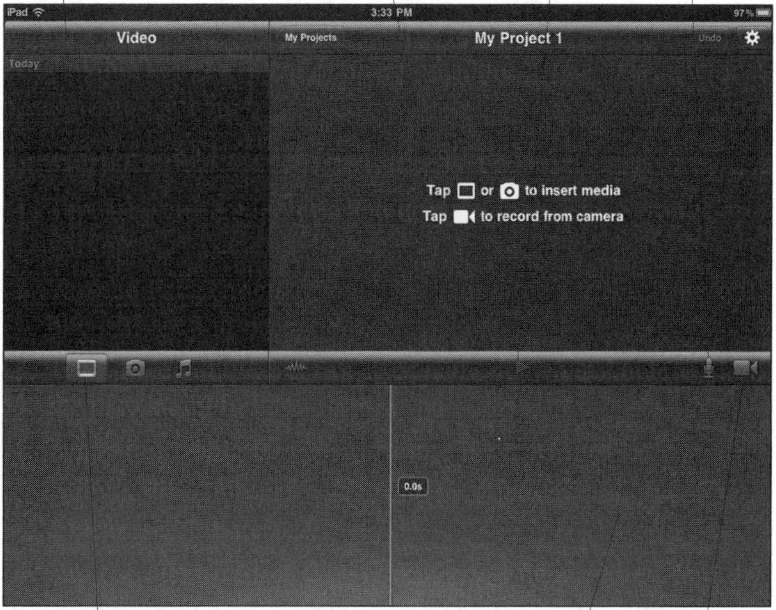

Mode controls   Timeline   Record video

Figure 11.9
*Recording
video from
iMovie.*

Record/stop button

Figure 11.10

Review your clip to make sure it's okay.

Tap the Play button to view the clip again, if need be. If the clip doesn't quite work, tap the Retake button to delete the clip and open the record video screen again. If the clip is acceptable, tap the Use button, which will open the project-editing screen once more (see Figure 11.11).

Figure 11.11

The project-editing screen with content.

The video clip you have recorded is now in the clips section, and the clip has been selected automatically so it appears in the monitor and timeline sections.

Working in the Cutting Room

The iMovie app is a fairly sophisticated tool that features a lot of editing capabilities. To give you a broad overview of how this interface works, here's how to put together a quick movie with a title screen and some music.

To put together a movie with a title screen and music:

1. Swipe the clip in the timeline so the viewing cursor is at the beginning of the clip.

2. Double-tap the clip in the timeline. The timeline will be selected, and the Clip Settings pop-over menu will appear (see Figure 11.12).

Figure 11.12

Every clip has its own properties.

3. Tap the Title Style option. The Title Style pop-over menu will open (see Figure 11.13).

Figure 11.13

Select a title.

4. Tap Opening. The option will be selected, and placeholder text will appear in the monitor, as seen in Figure 11.14.

Figure 11.14

Enter title text.

5. Tap the Title Text Here placeholder. A keyboard will appear for you to enter a title.

6. Enter a new title and tap Done on the keyboard. The new title will be entered.

7. Tap the Audio mode button. The Audio screen will open, as seen in Figure 11.15.

Figure 11.15

Select your own soundtrack.

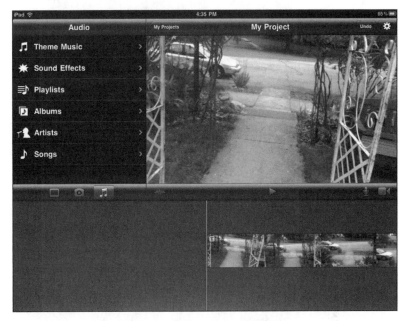

8. Tap the Theme Music option. The Theme Music list will appear.

9. Tap the option that appeals to you. The music will be overlaid on the timeline clip.

10. Tap the Play button to hear the clip. If the music isn't what you want, tap another option to try it instead.

TIP   **Use Your Own Tunes**

You can also use your own music from the iPad as the audio track for your movie. See Chapter 10, "Entertainment with iTunes," for more information on how to purchase or import music to your iPad.

11. When your movie is ready, tap the My Projects control. It will now appear in the My Projects window.

12. To change the name of the project, double-tap the name of the project in the project marquee. Use the keyboard to edit the project name (see Figure 11.16).

Figure 11.16

Display your project proudly.

There is a lot more to iMovie than this; we've only just scratched the surface. The app's Help system, available in the My Projects screen, is very thorough, and can really help you edit your own movies.

Conclusion

Photography and video are a big part of our lives now, and with the iPad, you have a one-size-fits-all device for quickly producing images and videos of your own.

Sometimes, you may want to get these images and other content printed on paper. This is something that's easy to do with the iPad, and in Chapter 12, "Printing with the iPad," we'll show you how to do it.

Chapter 12
Printing with the iPad

When the iPad was first introduced, many industry watchers wondered aloud, "How will users be able to print from the iPad?" (There are people who actually get paid to think up questions like this.)

In the beginning, third-party vendors would step up to provide solutions that would provide printing functionality from nearly every iPad app that could utilize it. The best of these, to date, is PrintCentral by EuroSmartz.

With the release of iOS 4.2, Apple itself added AirPrint functionality to the iPad (and the later-released iPad 2). AirPrint will seamlessly connect to any AirPrint-compatible printer on your network, without any configuration steps.

In this chapter, you will find out how to:

* Print from most apps with AirPrint functionality
* Connect to printers on your local network
* Print emails, contacts, and Web pages from your iPad

Print with AirPrint

If you are fortunate enough to have a printer that's compatible with the AirPrint system, then whenever your iPad is in the same network as such a printer, you can print directly to that printer.

Currently, there are 102 printers that will work with AirPrint, from five major printer manufacturers:

* Brother
* Canon
* EPSON
* Hewlett Packard
* Lexmark

Over 100 printers is a lot to choose from, so you should be able to find a printer model that meets your needs and is AirPrint-compatible. If you have one of these printers and it is correctly set up on your network, then printing is very simple.

In most apps, you will find the Print function in the Share action menu—the idea being that users are "sharing" the screen content when they print it. There are exceptions, of course, so you may need to look around in your app for the Print command.

Once you locate the Print command in your app, it's a simple matter to print.

To print with AirPrint:

1. Tap the Print command. The Printer Options action menu will open (see Figure 12.1).

Figure 12.1

The Printer Options action menu.

2. If a printer is not available, tap the Select Printer option. The Printer action menu will open, listing all compatible printers in that network (see Figure 12.2).

Figure 12.2

Viewing available and compatible printers.

3. Tap the printer you want to use. The Printer Options action menu will reappear.

4. Tap Print. The page will be sent to the assigned printer.

NOTE   Not Exactly Speedy

You may notice that printing jobs sent from the iPad are a bit slower than when you are printing from your computer. That's because much of the work done to prepare the content for the printer is done on the printer, instead of the iPad. That means the printer has to do more work, and a lot more connection time is used to send content across the network to the printer.

If you have one of the few printers that doesn't have AirPrint capabilities, don't fret; with PrintCentral, you can print to nearly any printer in your home.

Set Up Printers with PrintCentral

After you install PrintCentral, you may be able to print directly to a printer immediately, if the printer is connected directly to your home network.

"Connected directly to your home network" is a concept that should be clearly defined.

There are two ways of connecting a printer to a network. The first way is to share a local computer, which is a printer connected to your computer, which is set to allows other users (or your iPad) to use it remotely. The advantage of this method is that it enables users to get to older printers that can't be directly connected to the network. The disadvantage is that the computer to which the shared printer is attached must be turned on for the printer to be used.

The other method is the direct network connection, where the printer has no connections to any computer, only the network, either through a network cable or WiFi. This method is preferred because the access to the printer is usually better. Most new printers have this feature, and you can easily connect them to your WiFi network in your home.

PrintCentral enables you to make use of either type of connection, as you will see.

The instructions in this chapter are, perhaps, the most technical in this book, but don't be challenged. By following the steps outlined in the next few sections, you should be able to get your printer talking to the iPad.

Network Printers

If your printer is directly connected to a network, and your iPad is connected wirelessly to that same network, you may discover PrintCentral has automatically done the configuration for you.

To connect PrintCentral to a networked printer:

1. Tap the PrintCentral app icon. PrintCentral will start with an initial notification dialog.

NOTE **What Browser?**

Because few iPad apps, if any, provide options to print, PrintCentral's clever solution is to provide its own tools from which users can print. Need to print a Web page? Don't use Safari; use PrintCentral's browser.

2. Tap the option that appeals to you. PrintCentral will open to the Documents screen (see Figure 12.3).

Figure 12.3

The Documents screen in PrintCentral.

3. To check to see if a networked printer has been configured, tap the Getting Started file. The contents of the file will appear in the preview window.

4. Tap the Printer icon. The Print dialog box will open, as seen in Figure 12.4.

5. Tap Choose. The Printers dialog box will open (see Figure 12.5).

6. If you see the network printer you want to use, tap the printer option. The printer will be added to the Print dialog, and the Printer setup dialog box will appear immediately (see Figure 12.6).

7. Confirm that the printer is connected correctly and tap the Test button. A printer test page will print, and you will be asked to confirm the operation.

Figure 12.4

The Print dialog box.

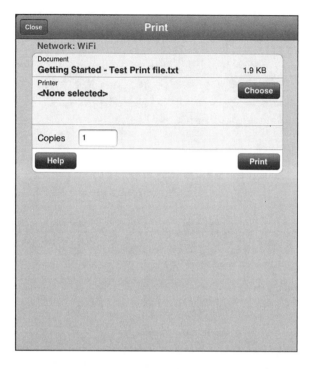

Figure 12.5

The Printers dialog box.

Figure 12.6

The Printer setup dialog box.

8. Tap Yes if the test page printed. The network printer is configured correctly.

If the network printer you want to use did not show up within the Printer dialog box, you can still add it.

To add a network printer:

1. Following the previous steps to get to the Printers dialog box, tap the Add Printer button. The Add Printer dialog box will appear, and you will be reminded to use the WePrint application.

2. Tap Continue to close the reminder dialog and then tap the Printer tab to view the Add Printer page (see Figure 12.7).

3. Enter the IP address of the printer to which you want to connect.

4. Enter a name for the printer in the Nickname field.

5. Tap Connect. The printer should be found and added to the Printers dialog box.

Figure 12.7

The Add Printer dialog box.

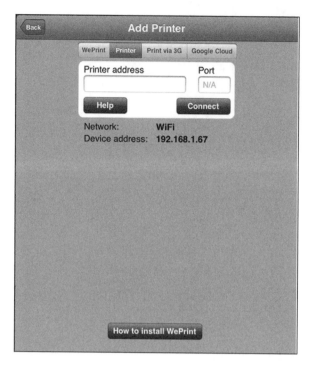

WePrint for Wi-Fi

Even if you have a networked printer, you can improve the quality of your print jobs by installing WePrint client software on your Mac or PC. WePrint acts as a printer server, which accepts printing jobs from your iPad and sends them to the printer connected to a computer on your network, either locally or via the network.

For users who do not have a network printer, WePrint is a required tool to use PrintCentral, because only through WePrint can your iPad reach the printer. But, if you already have your printer connected to the network, and have completed the steps in the previous section, you may be asking yourself why you would need to use WePrint. The short answer is quality.

When PrintCentral communicates directly with a networked printer, it uses software on your iPad to send a "generic" print job to that printer. This is done to save room on the iPad, because installing the printer software for every possible printer would eat up a lot of iPad storage. So your print jobs will be adequate, but not the best quality.

WePrint takes advantage of the fact that your computer already has the best software to use for your printer—it has to, otherwise you wouldn't be able to print from your PC or Mac. With WePrint, a print job is sent from the iPad to the WePrint software, which then hands off the job to your computer's printer software, which, in turn, sends it to the printer in the best format.

This may sound convoluted, but unless your network is under a very heavy traffic load, print jobs from the iPad via WePrint take very little extra time. Best of all, the WePrint software is free to download and install from http://mobile.eurosmartz.com/downloads/downloads_index.html.

Installing WePrint is no different than installing any other Windows or OS X application. You will be asked, during installation, if you want to allow WePrint to communicate outside of your computer's firewall. You will need to say yes; otherwise, your iPad will be blocked from handing off print jobs to WePrint.

After WePrint is installed and running on your computer, make a note of the Server Address and Port information shown on the Status page of the WePrint application (see Figure 12.8). You will need this information to configure the printer in PrintCentral.

Figure 12.8

The WePrint application.

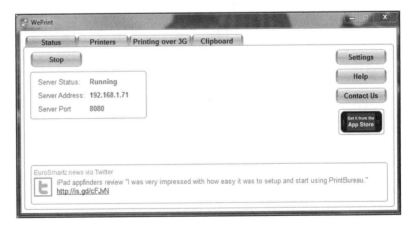

To use WePrint to connect to a printer:

1. In the Printers dialog box, tap the Printing over WiFi option. The Add Printer dialog box will appear, and you will be reminded to use the WePrint application.

2. Tap Continue to close the reminder dialog.

3. Enter the IP address of the WePrint Server to which you want to connect (it was shown in Figure 12.8).

4. Enter a name for the server in the Nickname field.

5. Tap Connect. All printers on the WePrint computer should be found and added to the Printers dialog box.

Printing

Once you have the printer configuration set, you can now start printing. As mentioned earlier in this chapter, PrintCentral does not enable printing in existing iPad apps. Instead, it duplicates the functions of some of the more useful apps and lets you print content from PrintCentral.

Files

You may have a lot of files on your iPad that need to be printed at any given time. Some of them will be on your iPad, and some will be on your computer. With some easy configuration, you can use PrintCentral to handle them all.

When you use PrintCentral to print a file, it will print documents to which PrintCentral has access.

To print from PrintCentral:

1. In PrintCentral, tap the Files tab. The Documents screen will appear.

2. Tap the file you want to print. The contents of the file will appear in the preview window.

3. Tap the Printer icon. The Print dialog box will open.

4. Type the number of copies you want to print.

5. Tap Print. The document will be printed.

Email

Printing email messages and their attachments can also be done in PrintCentral. All you need to do is set up your account information, which PrintCentral can use to pick up copies of the messages in your Inbox.

To print email:

1. In PrintCentral, tap the Email tab. The Email Accounts screen will appear.

2. Tap the Add a new account option. An accounts dialog box will appear.

3. Tap the account type you need. The Edit Account screen will open.

4. Type the settings for your email account and then tap Test. If the settings are correct, a green check mark will indicate your success.

5. Tap the Email Accounts navigation control to return to the Email Accounts screen.

6. Tap the email account from which to print. The account's mailbox page will open (see Figure 12.9).

Figure 12.9

An example of a multifoldered account.

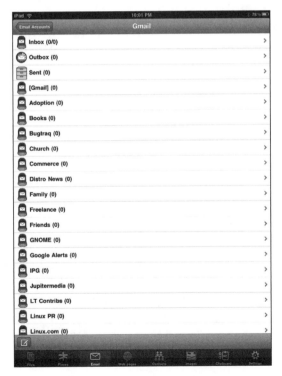

7. Tap the mailbox folder that contains the message you want to print. The contents of the folder will be downloaded.

8. Tap the message you want to print. The contents of the message will appear in the preview window.

9. Tap the Printer icon. The Print dialog box will open.

10. Type the number of copies you want to print.

11. Tap Print. The message will be printed.

TIP   Printing Attachments

If an email message has an attachment, click the attachment to open it within PrintCentral. Then click the Printer icon to start the printing process. You can use this method to mail yourself a document as an attachment and print it in PrintCentral.

Web Pages

In the previous "Email" section, you learned how to use emails to get documents set up for printing. For Web pages, though, you have to use different ways of printing. Here's how to handle different settings for Web pages in PrintCentral.

To print Web pages in PrintCentral:

1. In PrintCentral, tap the Web Pages tab. The browser will open.

2. Navigate to the Web page you want to print. The page will open in the PrintCentral browser window.

TIP   Quick Navigation

If you find a page to print while using Safari, select the Web address in the URL bar and use the Edit menu to copy the address. Paste it into the PrintCentral browser's URL bar to get to the same page fast.

---

3. Tap the PrintCentral Printer icon. The Print action menu will appear.

4. To print a screenshot of the page, tap the Print from Screen option. To print the contents of the page, tap the Print from Address option. The Print dialog box will open.

5. Type the number of copies you want to print.

6. Tap Print. The Web page will be printed.

Contacts

Want to print out the information on one or more of your contacts? PrintCentral will connect you right to the Contacts data on your iPad and print them out as needed.

To print out information on your contacts:

1. In PrintCentral, tap the Contacts tab. The Contacts Groups screen will open.

2. Tap the group with the contact you want to print. The list of contacts will appear.

3. Tap the contact(s) to print. Each selected contact will be marked with a check mark.

4. Tap the Printer icon. The Print dialog box will open.

5. Type the number of copies you want to print.

6. Tap Print. The contact(s) will be printed.

Images

If you need to print a copy of the images on your iPad, here's how to do it.

To print a copy of your images:

1. In PrintCentral, tap the Images tab. The Photos screen will open, as well as the Photo Albums action menu (see Figure 12.10).

2. Tap the album with the image you want to print. A gallery of images will appear in the action menu.

3. Tap the image to print. Each selected image will appear in the Photos screen.

4. Tap the Printer icon. The Print dialog box will open.

5. Type the number of copies you want to print.

6. Tap Print. The image(s) will be printed.

Clipboard

Sometimes you may need to print just a portion of a document, instead of the whole thing. You can use the iPad's editing tools to copy a selection to the iPad Clipboard and then print the selection from PrintCentral.

To print a Clipboard selection with PrintCentral:

1. In PrintCentral, tap the Clipboard tab. The Clip archive screen will open (see Figure 12.11).

2. Tap the clipboard items to select or deselect. Selected items will be denoted by a check mark.

3. Tap the Printer icon. The Print dialog box will open.

4. Type the number of copies you want to print.

5. Tap Print. The selected content will be printed.

Figure 12.11

The archived content of the clipboard.

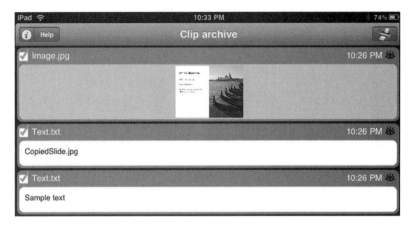

Conclusion

In this chapter, you discovered that printing from the iPad is not a myth but a reality, and it can be a valuable tool for your iPad use.

In Chapter 13, "Keeping Track of Friends and Family," you'll find out how the iPad can help you work with the popular Facebook application to keep in touch with the ones you love.

Chapter 13
Keeping Track of Friends and Family

They have weird names, like Facebook, YouTube, Flickr, and Twitter—websites and services that provide something invaluable: a connection.

All of these site are known as *social media sites*, and they provide ways for you to share your life with friends and family. Just as communication can happen through email on your iPad, you can get even more connections using a social media service.

In this chapter, you'll look at an important app that will help create the conversation on one of the most popular social media sites today: Facebook. Specifically, you'll learn how to:

❋ Create a Facebook account

❋ Use the Facebook iPad app

Setting Up a Facebook Account

It's pretty hard not to have heard of Facebook, the social media site that enables friends, family, and colleagues to connect with each other.

Facebook is not the first social media site, but through tight management of undesirable content and general protection of its users' privacy, it has grown to be the largest. It is not without its flaws. Those same privacy rules have become weaker as Facebook explores ways to generate revenue for itself and its partner vendors. Time will tell how this issue will resolve itself, but for now, Facebook is definitely a place to connect.

To begin to build your connections to family and friends on Facebook, you will need to set up your own Facebook account. You can do this using the official Facebook app, which you will need to download and install.

To set up a Facebook account:

1. Start the Facebook app. The login page will appear, as shown in Figure 13.1.

Figure 13.1

The Facebook login page.

2. Tap the Sign Up for Facebook button. The Safari app will open to the Facebook account creation page (see Figure 13.2).

3. Fill in the fields on the page and tap the Sign Up button. Facebook will then step you through any remaining steps for setup.

Figure 13.2

Create your Facebook account.

NOTE **The Ever-Changing Setup**

You will need to step through the rest of Facebook's setup process on your own. That's because this process is something that Facebook is constantly refining, and it's never entirely clear what the exact steps will be. One word of advice: avoid giving permissions to any apps (like games) to access your account until you are familiar with Facebook. This is not just a security issue; it's a nuisance issue.

Getting Friendly with Facebook

Facebook's basic idea works something like this: You, as a Facebook user, can connect to friends (which can include family and professional colleagues) who, in turn, will connect back to you, while also connecting to their circle of friends, thus expanding the network to a very large, interconnected set of relationships.

Facebook users participate in different ways, updating their status at various intervals, promoting events, sending messages, sharing photos, or engaging in live chats with friends who are online at the same time. Not all of the activities on Facebook are geared toward socializing; there are games, polls, and other diverting activities that can keep you engaged, should you want to participate.

The Facebook app acts as a direct gateway to many of the social activities on Facebook, though not the entertainment aspects. If you want to play the many games and other diverting activities on Facebook, it's best to use a computer to log into your account. But to connect with your loved ones, the Facebook app is perfect.

Once you have logged into your Facebook account with the Facebook app, you will see an interface similar to that found on the actual Facebook site. The News Feed on the Home screen is shown in Figure 13.3.

Figure 13.3

The News Feed shows what's happening with friends and family right now.

At the top left of the app, you will see a small menu switch. Tap that switch, and the other pages you can access will be displayed.

Tap the Events option to view the latest events your friends and family have sent out. If you want to view older events, tap events in the Past Events section (see Figure 13.4).

Figure 13.4

Viewing events, upcoming and past.

The Nearby option will enable you to check in and broadcast your current location and view your friends' locations if they've opted to share that information. You may want to be careful with this sort of information, because location privacy is something you want to strongly manage for personal safety reasons.

If you tap your personal icon, you will see the Profile screen, which displays the Wall, Info, Photos, and Friends pages. The Wall page, shown in Figure 13.5, shows your status updates and any public messages that anyone has written to you.

Figure 13.5

*A look at
your Wall.*

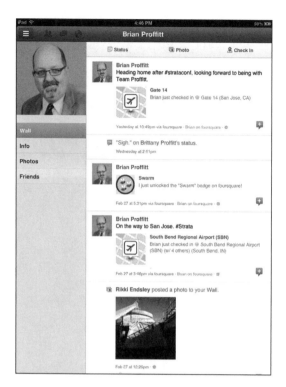

The Info page will show your personal information that you have opted to share with your friends and family; the Photos page will display any images you have uploaded to Facebook, or images you're in that your friends have tagged with your name; and the Friends page will display a pictorial directory of your friends.

> **NOTE** **Photo Management**
>
> At this time, the Facebook app can view, tag, and save photos in a Facebook account.

Once your friends and family find you on Facebook (which you can help along by letting them know on your own), they will be able to write messages to you on your Wall.

To respond to a comment:

1. To respond to a comment from a friend or family member, tap the Comment icon underneath the message. The Write a comment sidebar will appear.

2. Type a reply to the comment and tap Send. Your reply will appear next to the original post by the friend, and Facebook will notify them of your reply.

TIP **Privacy Is Precious**

One thing that doesn't always occur to Facebook users... try not to mention when you are away from home on Facebook (or any social media site, for that matter). Savvy criminals could see that you are posting away from your home and take the opportunity to visit your home with burglary in mind. Be discrete with your comings and goings.

Another way to communicate with your friends is using Facebook chat, a real-time text exchange. This only works if the friend has actually "friended" you personally. If they have, you can chat with them if you are online at the same time as they are.

To use Facebook chat:

1. Tap the Messages icon in the top toolbar of the Facebook app. The Messages action menu will open (see Figure 13.6).

2. To start a conversation, tap a friend in the list, which displays anyone who is online. A chat window will be displayed in the action menu (see Figure 13.7).

3. Tap the chat field and enter the start of a conversation, tapping Send when your comment is complete.

4. Continue the conversation until its conclusion. Tap anywhere on the screen, when finished, to close the action menu.

Figure 13.6

Chatting with friends.

Figure 13.7

Starting a chat.

Conclusion

The power of social media is very useful when you want to reach out to those people who are important in your life. Facebook is an excellent way to connect, and the iPad Facebook app is a great Facebook tool.

In Chapter 14, "Managing Your Life," we'll see how the iPad will let you organize the one thing we never seem to have enough of: time.

Chapter 14
Managing Your Life

One of the best things the iPad enables you to do is keep track of your busy schedule and the people in your life. This makes sense, since that was the main job of the earliest handheld electronic devices that preceded the iPad. Instead of an address book or a date book, you could carry around the electronic version, all in one plastic device.

As the devices got smaller and faster, that basic job never went away. As our lives get busier and full with more and more people we'd like to meet again someday, the need to keep track of all those faces and dates is still important.

Thus, it's no surprise that the iPad features two apps that manage people and events in your life. Contacts is the easy-to-use address book, and Calendar is the straightforward scheduling app that lets you track your busy life and all your family appointments as well.

In this chapter, you will learn how to do the following:

✳ Add friends and family information to the Contacts app

✳ Manage your schedule with the Calendar app

Navigating Contacts

Many iPad apps have a lot of flash and sparkle designed to ooo! and ahh! users as they work through the app.

Contacts is very much *not* one of those apps.

This is not to downplay its importance. Indeed, you may not realize it, but Contacts is one of the most important apps on the iPad. That's because whenever any of the other apps needs to connect you to someone you might know, the Contacts app is the only place they look.

The Contacts app is simple for one main reason: It should not be difficult to manage an address book. If you look at Figure 14.1, you can see the simple Contacts interface for yourself.

Figure 14.1

The main Contacts screen.

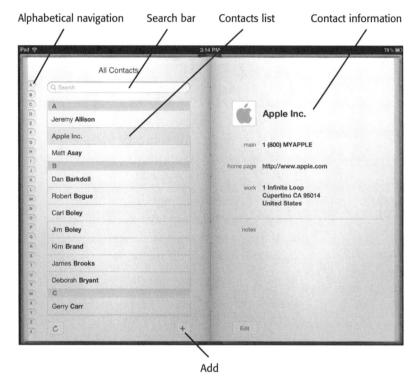

Alphabetical navigation   Search bar   Contacts list   Contact information

Add

> ## TIP   The Best Way to View Contacts (and Calendar)
>
> While you can view Contacts and Calendar in Portrait mode, you may find it better to rotate the iPad 90 degrees and use the apps in Landscape mode. This mode gives the apps more of a book-like view, which is what the designers were going for.

To navigate in Contacts, tap and drag the list of contacts on the left "page" to scroll up and down the page. Or tap the letter icon for the last name of the person you want to view, and the contacts list will immediately move to that letter of the alphabet.

This simple interface is simple all the way through, as you will see.

Managing Contacts

When you use Contacts, the very first thing you will need to do is add a contact of your own to the contacts list.

To add your own contact:

1. In Contacts, tap the Add button. The Info page will appear (see Figure 14.2).

Figure 14.2

Adding a new contact.

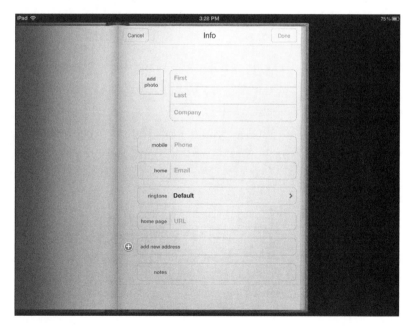

2. Tap the First field. The cursor will appear in that field.
3. Type the first name of the person you are adding.

4. Repeat Steps 2–3 for all of the other fields on the page. Fields of interest include:

- **Ringtone.** You can tap this option to bring up a list of rings to associate with the person you are contacting. This is more useful for the iPhone version of this app, but if you are sharing information with an iPhone of your own, you can set this option on the iPad.

- **Home page.** If the person you are entering has a blog or a Web page of her own, you can enter the Web address here.

- **Add new address.** If there is a mailing address you want to add to the contact, tap the green Add icon to bring up additional address fields.

- **Add field.** If you don't see a field you want to put information in (such as a Suffix field for "Jr.", tap the Add Field button to display the Add Field pop-over list.

5. When you are finished entering information, tap the Done button. The contact will be added.

To remove a contact from the Contacts app:

1. In Contacts, tap the contact you want to remove. The contact's page will appear.

2. Tap the Edit button. The Info page for the contact will appear.

3. Scroll down to the bottom of the Info page and tap the Delete Contact button. A confirmation dialog will appear (see Figure 14.3).

Figure 14.3

Removing a contact.

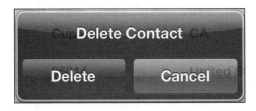

4. Tap Delete. The contact will be removed from the contacts list.

Navigating Calendar

Like Contacts, the Calendar app is a model of simplicity. This is a good thing, since managing your schedule can be a complex business on its own.

As you can see in Figure 14.4, the Calendar app has a similar look and feel to the Contacts app, but it adds a few more controls.

Figure 14.4

The main Calendar screen.

Calendars   Invitations   View controls   Search bar

Current month

Today's event agenda

Today's schedule

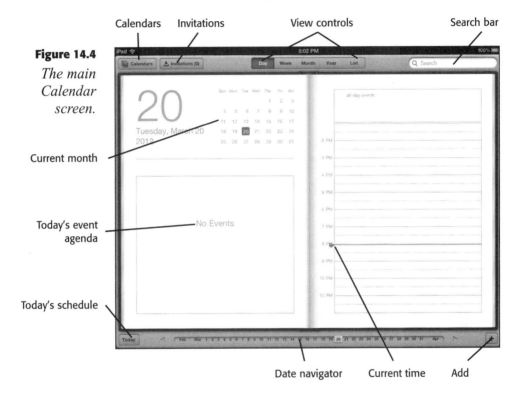

Date navigator   Current time   Add

Some of the elements highlighted in Figure 14.4 are self-explanatory, but there are a few key features that should be explained a bit further.

The View controls, for instance, let you select how you want to see your events. The Day view shown in the previous figure is the default view for Calendar, but if you tap the Week button, you will see the Calendar display an entire week's worth of events (see Figure 14.5).

Figure 14.5

*The Calendar
Week view.*

The List view is unique, compared to the other date-oriented views. Displayed in Figure 14.6, the List view will display an entire month's worth of information for you in a list rather than inside a calendar.

Figure 14.6

*The Calendar
List view.*

Tapping on the appointments in the Agenda view on the left will open the Schedule for that appointment's given day. It's a handy view to use when you are reviewing a lot of events on your calendar.

In the Day view, there are two parts of the screen that would seem to be similar: the Agenda and the Schedule. But, as you can see in Figure 14.7, each section has its own way of showing your daily events.

Figure 14.7

The Agenda and the Schedule.

The Agenda view on the left displays your daily itinerary in simple list form. The Schedule on the right shows the day in hourly blocks and displays the events in the Calendar in relation to each other. This is very useful to tell at a glance if two appointments may be in conflict or too close together.

Along the bottom of the screen is the Date navigator. You can flip through days, weeks, or months by flicking the pages, just as you learned to do in the iBook app in Chapter 9, "iBooks for Reading." Or you can tap and drag along the Date navigator to display a popover menu that will show the date that your finger is resting upon (see Figure 14.8).

Figure 14.8

*Using the
Date
navigator.*

Once you find the date you want to open, lift your finger, and the Calendar will open to that date.

Now that the basics of the Calendar have been examined, it's time to start learning how to organize your life with the app.

Managing Events

In order to use Calendar, you will need to know how to perform the basic operation of adding events to the app.

To add an event to the Calendar:

1. In the Calendar app, tap the Add button. The Add Event action menu will appear, as shown in Figure 14.9.

2. Tap the Title field and type a description of the event or appointment.

3. Tap the Location field and type a location for the appointment.

4. To change the time and date for the event, tap the Starts Ends option. The Start & End action menu will appear (see Figure 14.10).

5. Flick the date rotation control until it reaches the date you want.

Figure 14.9

Adding an event.

Figure 14.10

The Start & End action menu.

6. Flick the hour and minute rotational controls until they match the time you desire.

7. Tap the Ends field and repeat Steps 5 and 6.

8. Tap Done. The Add Event action menu will reappear.

9. If you want to add a reminder to the event, tap the Alert option. The Event Alert action menu will appear.

10. Tap the time before the event you want the reminder to appear.

11. Tap Done. The Add Event action menu will reappear.

12. Tap Done. The event will appear in the Calendar on the date and time you specified (see Figure 14.11).

Figure 14.11

The new event.

NOTE   **A Faster Way to Add Events**

If you navigate to the date and time of the event in the Calendar, you can long-press the Schedule at the time you want the event to start. The Add Event action menu will appear with a one-hour block of time already set for that start time.

Sometimes, you will have events that will repeat at regular intervals, such as a weekly commitment to volunteer at a local charity. You don't have to enter the event separately for each week—just create a recurring event.

To add a recurring event:

1. In the Calendar app, tap the Add button. The Add Event action menu will appear.

2. Tap the Title field and type a description of the event or appointment.

3. Tap the Location field and type a location for the appointment.

4. To change the time and date for the event, tap the Starts Ends option. The Start & End action menu will appear.

5. Flick the date rotation control until it reaches the date you want.

6. Flick the hour and minute rotational controls until they match the time you desire.

7. Tap the Ends field and repeat Steps 5 and 6.

8. Tap Done. The Add Event action menu will reappear.

9. Tap the Repeat option. The Repeat action menu will appear (see Figure 14.12).

Figure 14.12

The Repeat action menu.

10. Tap the interval that you want the event to repeat.

11. Tap Done. The Add Event action menu will reappear.

12. If you want to add a reminder to the recurring event, tap the Alert option. The Event Alert action menu will appear.

13. Tap the time before the recurring event you want the reminder to appear.

14. Tap Done. The Add Event action menu will reappear.

15. Tap Done. The recurring event will appear in the Calendar on the dates and time you specified.

Some events are more free-form in their scheduling, such as a family reunion or wedding. You can set up all-day events in the Calendar to mark just the date for the big days.

To add an all-day event:

1. In the Calendar app, tap the Add button. The Add Event action menu will appear.

2. Tap the Title field and type a description of the event or appointment.

3. Tap the Location field and type a location for the appointment.

4. To change the time and date for the event, tap the Starts Ends option. The Start & End action menu will appear.

5. Slide the All-day control to On. The rotational controls will change to month, day, and year controls.

6. Flick the rotational controls until they match the date you desire.

7. Tap Done. The Add Event action menu will reappear.

8. If you want to add a reminder to the all-day event, tap the Alert option. The Event Alert action menu will appear.

9. Tap the time before the all-day event you want the reminder to appear.

10. Tap Done. The Add Event action menu will reappear.

11. Tap Done. The all-day event will appear in the Calendar on the date you specified.

To edit any existing event, simply tap the event on the Schedule. The Edit action menu will appear, from which you can change any aspect of the event.

If an appointment gets cancelled completely, you can easily remove the event.

To remove an event:

1. Long-press the event you want to remove. The Add Event action menu will appear.

2. Scroll to the bottom of the menu and tap the Delete Event button. A confirmation button will appear.

3. Tap the Delete Event button again. The event will be removed from the Calendar.

Manage Calendars

One of the very nice features of Calendar is the capability to manage multiple calendars within the app. This is extremely useful if you have more than one person in your household that you need to schedule. You can have a calendar for you and a separate one for your significant other, which will help coordinate events and reduce schedule conflicts.

To create a new calendar:

1. Tap the Calendars button. The Show Calendars action menu will appear.

2. Tap the Edit button. The Edit Calendars action menu will appear.

3. Tap the Add Calendars option. The Add Calendar action menu will appear (see Figure 4.13).

Figure 14.13

The Add Calendar action menu.

4. Tap the Untitled Calendar field and enter a name for the new calendar.

5. Tap a color you want to assign the calendar.

6. Tap Done. The Edit Calendars action menu will reappear.

7. Tap outside the Edit Calendars action menu. The menu will close, and the new calendar will appear as an option whenever you add a new event to the app.

Conclusion

Your life can be pretty busy sometimes, so it's extremely useful to manage your schedule and your contacts with the iPad.

Sometimes, you will want to just get away from it all and break free of those schedules. But even as you travel, the iPad can still be of great use to you, as you'll see in Chapter 15, "On the Go with the iPad."

Chapter 15
On the Go with the iPad

Travel is more a part of our lives than ever. Never in history has it been easier for people to journey across states, countries, and even oceans to see what there is to see. If the Internet has made the world a smaller place, then it has also served to increase our desire to go out and see the world for ourselves.

The iPad is an almost perfect travel companion. Besides all of the apps outlined in this book (and more), the lightweight form factor makes it ideal for planes, trains, and automobiles.

The travel benefits of the iPad start even before you leave on your trip. Two great apps can help you plan and track your trip in real time: Kayak and FlightTrack Pro. And once you're away from your home, you can easily access data (music, movies, and apps) from Apple's new iCloud service. In this chapter, you'll learn how to:

* Search for the best travel deals using Kayak
* Make reservations for air, hotel, and rental cars
* Track any flight in the world live with FlightTrack Pro
* Connect to Apple's iCloud service
* Sync information across multiple devices
* Back up your iPad to iCloud
* Safeguard your iPad device and data

Now Boarding: Kayak

Perhaps the industry that has benefited the most from the Internet is the travel industry, although you might have a hard time selling travel agents on that. There are dozens of travel websites providing the self-service capability to book travel and accommodations.

In the U.S. alone, Expedia, Hotwire, and Priceline are just a few of the big travel sites providing this service.

With such diversity, a valid question becomes, which one gives you the best rates?

Kayak is an app that makes the answer to such a question moot. Kayak searches several travel sites at once and reports back all the fares and rates it finds—letting you find and book a flight, hotel stay, or rental car from one easy interface.

Searching for a Flight

Kayak features a comprehensive interface for flight searching that lets you see most of your trip options on a single screen. This enables you to change these options at a glance, which makes searching for possible flights a lot easier than backing up to another screen on your browser to make changes.

To find a flight on Kayak:

1. Tap the KAYAK app icon. Kayak will open to the Explore screen, with Boston as the default city (see Figure 15.1).

Figure 15.1

The initial Kayak Explore screen.

2. Tap the Flights button. The Flights screen will appear, as seen in Figure 15.2.

Figure 15.2
The Flights screen.

3. To start the flight search, tap the From field. The Choose Origin Airport pane will appear (see Figure 15.3).

4. Tap the Current location option or type the name of a city in the From Airport search box and tap the corresponding airport option. The airport will appear in the From field.

NOTE   **Airport Codes**

Savvy travelers know the airport code for their home airport, having seen it on their baggage claim tags so many times. Los Angeles, for instance, is LAX, and New York's LaGuardia airport is LGA. You can enter that three-letter code in any field and Kayak can use it.

Figure 15.3

*The Choose
Origin
Airport pane.*

5. Tap the To field. The Choose Destination Airport pane will appear.

6. Tap the Current location option or type the name of a city in the To Airport search box and tap the corresponding airport option. The airport will appear in the To field.

7. Tap the Depart field. The Depart action menu will appear.

8. Tap the date of departure. The departure date will appear in the Depart field.

9. Tap the Return field. The Return action menu will appear.

10. Tap the date of return. The return date will appear in the Return field.

11. Tap the + or – icons in the Travelers field to set the number of passengers on the trip, if needed.

12. To change the class, tap the Cabin button. The Select Class pop-over will appear.

13. Tap the desired class option.

14. Tap the Search button. Kayak will search for the flights that match your criteria, from lowest to highest fare (see Figure 15.4).

Figure 15.4
Found flights.

After the initial search, you may want to start looking for options beyond price, such as when the flight leaves and arrives, or how many stops the flight makes. Depending on the frequent flyer mile program you might belong to, you may want to select certain airlines over others.

When Kayak displays results, it uses filters to parse out which results are shown to you. By default, all filters are selected when results are initially displayed so that the most results are shown. You can navigate through the Filter pane and tap different options to fine-tune the reported results.

For instance, tapping on the Airports tab in the Filter pane will show the airports involved in the trip. By tapping options, you can eliminate options, particularly in the Layover Airports category.

The Times option lets you set preferred times for take-off and departure on each leg of the trip. As you change any of the Filter pane options, you may see dramatic changes for the results of your search.

Booking a Flight

Once you get the times, airlines, and other flight parameters set, hopefully at a price you can handle, you can reserve the flight. Kayak doesn't actually reserve the flights but instead seamlessly connects you to the travel site on which it found the rate so you can complete the reservation there.

To reserve a flight through Kayak:

1. Tap the flight you want to book. The Flight Details action menu will appear, as seen in Figure 15.5.

Figure 15.5

Information about your flight.

2. Tap Book Now. Kayak will refer you to the site that provided that flight. If successful, Kayak will pass along all of the data it gathered about the flight to the third-party site, which should open to a booking page with the information already filled in (see Figure 15.6).

Figure 15.6

The travel site with your booking information.

3. Continue with the booking process on the travel site to complete the reservation.

Finding a Hotel

If you want to reserve a room at a hotel, you can still do that. Kayak handles hotel search and reservation operations with ease.

To search for a hotel and set up a reservation:

1. Tap the Hotel icon. The Search Hotels action menu will appear, as seen in Figure 15.7.

2. Enter the information for your stay in the appropriate fields and tap Search. After a few moments, the results of the search will be displayed.

3. When you find a hotel you want to reserve, tap the hotel's listing. A selection of booking options will appear in a pop-over (see Figure 15.8).

Figure 15.7

Searching for hotels.

Figure 15.8

Choose a booking site.

4. Tap the Book Online button for the site you want to use for reserving the room. The travel site will open and your pre-entered information will appear.

5. Continue with the booking process on the travel site to complete the reservation.

Get a Rental Car

As with reserving a hotel room or flights, Kayak can be used to complete the rental car reservation process.

To rent a car:

1. Tap the Rental Car icon. The Search Cars action menu will appear.

2. Enter the information for the car in the appropriate fields and tap Search. After a few moments, the results of the search will be displayed.

3. When you find a car you want to reserve, tap the Select button. The Choose a site pop-over will appear.

4. Tap the Book Now button for the travel site you want to use for reserving the car. The travel site will open and your pre-entered information will appear.

5. Continue with the booking process on the travel site to complete the reservation.

NOTE **Ready to Explore?**

If you're feeling adventurous, tap the Explore screen in Kayak and find out just how far you can go on a given fare. Just configure your location, dates, what you'd like to do, and how many stops you're willing to make, and Kayak will display all the possible destinations on the global map, shown in Figure 15.9. Tap on any orange dot to see details about the location and flights.

Figure 15.9

*Hawai'i, here
I come.*

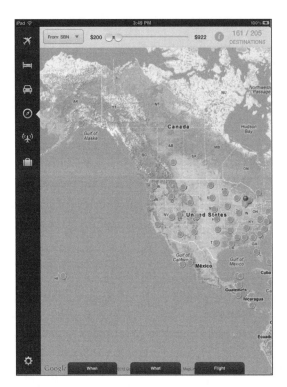

In-Flight: Tracking Your Flight

When you're facing security lines, luggage check-in, and other air-port headaches, the last thing you want to find out is that your flight has been delayed. The smallest delay can create a ripple effect on your entire travel plans, and if you're going to miss a con-nection or your ride from the airport will be delayed, the faster you know, the faster you can react.

FlightTrack Pro is the app that will help you track any flight you need, whether it's next week's business trip or your mother-in-law's incoming flight. Every flight is important in its own way.

Setting up FlightTrack Pro is simple—all you need is the flight number for the flight you're tracking and the date of departure.

To search for and save flights:

1. Tap the FlightTrack app icon. FlightTrack Pro will open (see Figure 15.10).

Figure 15.10

The initial FlightTrack Pro screen.

2. Tap the Add icon. The Add Flight action menu will appear (see Figure 15.11).

Figure 15.11

The Add Flight action menu.

3. Tap the Airline field. The Airline action menu will appear.

4. Type the airline name. Matching airline options will appear in the menu.

5. Tap the appropriate airline. The Search action menu will reappear.

6. Type the flight number in the Flight # field.

7. Tap the Departs field. The Departure Date action menu will appear.

8. Enter the date of departure and tap Search. The Add Flight action menu will reappear.

9. Tap Search in the Add Flight action menu. Possible matches will appear in the Flights action menu (see Figure 15.12).

Figure 15.12

The Flights action menu.

10. Tap the flight you want. The flight's action menu will appear (see Figure 15.13).

11. Tap Save. A map of the plane's route and its position in flight will be displayed.

12. To view the status of the flight at any time, tap the plane on the map to see the flight's information.

Figure 15.13

The flight's information.

> **NOTE** **Flight Updates**
>
> As schedule changes to the flight are made, the changes will be updated with notification messages. Tap OK to close or View to view the flight's information in a pop-over menu.

FlightTrack Pro also enables users to connect to TripIt, a social network for travelers, so they can see who is traveling near them as they're on the go. For more information, or to connect to an existing TripIt account, tap the Flights button and then the Info icon.

Connecting to iCloud

iCloud is an online software service offered by Apple for users of any Apple device or any device that runs on Windows PCs if you have one.

You may have heard "the cloud" mentioned a lot on commercials and news reports. Many times, it's used as a descriptive term for the Internet, and loosely that's a close label. But it's not entirely correct.

The cloud is actually software that provides you with a service, just like any software on your computer, except with the cloud, the software is actually running on a computer somewhere else.

This is exactly what iCloud is: a service provided by Apple to you, Apple's customer. Alongside features like photo and file sharing, iCloud provides 5GB of storage on the cloud to start and the option to purchase more storage if needed.

Other tools include over-the-air email, a calendar, and contact synchronization across multiple devices. There's a feature that will let you find your iPad if you leave it behind somewhere and lock it down remotely to keep others from seeing your data.

All of these services can be of great benefit to you when you are away from home.

Signing up for iCloud can be done on any computer that can use the service, which includes your iPad.

To sign up for iCloud on the iPad:

1. Tap the Settings app icon. The Settings app will open.
2. Tap the iCloud option. The iCloud settings page will appear (see Figure 15.14).
3. Enter your Apple ID and Password in the appropriate fields. This is what you created when you first set up an iTunes account in Chapter 1, "First Step: Introducing the iPad."
4. Tap Sign In. The iCloud settings page will open, and a notification window will appear asking for permission to share your iPad's location (see Figure 15.15).
5. Tap OK. The settings page will be visible.

> **NOTE   No Matter Where You Go, There You Are**
>
> Apple is very protective of user privacy, so it will always ask you for permission when an application wants to share information, such as location, with Apple. In this case, the Find My iPad application is a very useful tool to have if your iPad is lost or stolen, and it's highly recommended that you allow this app to share the device's location with iCloud.

Figure 15.14

The iCloud settings page.

Figure 15.15

Do you want to share?

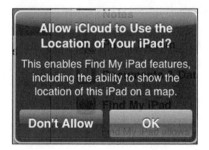

At this point, you will be able to pick and choose which of your iPad's core applications will be connected to iCloud. You might think, for instance, that all of your apps should be connected, but if you don't use the app in question, then there's really no need to waste bandwidth time having your iPad try to sync data that isn't even there.

Beyond the self-explanatory app settings, there are a few additional settings that can provide a lot of functionality should you choose to use them.

* **Photo Stream.** When activated, this tool will upload all new pictures from your iPad and will automatically synchronize them with any other iCloud-connected device you have.

* **Documents & Data.** This general setting enables any iCloud-enabled app not listed here in these settings to upload and save documents to iCloud's storage service.

* **Find My iPad.** Activates the Find My iPad locator service, discussed later in this chapter.

* **Storage & Backup.** Controls your backup settings for sending your iPad data to the iCloud service.

Synchronizing Across Multiple Devices

The beauty of using iCloud is having the capability to synchronize information such as contacts, Safari bookmarks, reminders, and calendar appointments. Not only will you be able to access the same information on any iCloud-enabled computer, but you can also log on to the iCloud site and see the same information from any computer or device with Internet capabilities, anywhere in the world.

If you want to use iCloud on one of your computers, you will first have to install it. (If you have an OS X machine with Lion (v10.7) or later, then iCloud is already available on your system.) Windows users can install the iCloud client found at www.apple.com/icloud/. iCloud is free to use, though if you need a lot of online storage, there is an annual subscription fee, as detailed in the "Back Up Your iPad to iCloud" section.

Once the iCloud software is installed, don't look for it as a program in your Windows Start Menu or OS X Dock. The client application is actually installed directly within your system preferences.

For OS X users, click the icon and then the System Preferences menu option, followed by the iCloud option.

In Windows, click the Start Menu and then click the Control Panel option. In the Control Panel window, click the Network and Internet link; then click the iCloud link.

Either of these methods will start the iCloud Preferences client, shown in Figures 15.16 and 15.17.

To change the iCloud configuration settings on any device, open the settings window in either the Windows or OS X configuration clients or within the iPad's Settings app. Then simply click the checkbox or slide the switch to begin synchronization of that particular service.

NOTE **Your First Time**

The first time you sync from a device to iCloud, a warning dialog box will appear. Click Allow to make sure all your data is captured and no duplicates are created.

To access your information online from iCloud at any time, just start a browser on any computer.

To access your information online from iCloud:

1. In your browser, navigate to www.icloud.com. The iCloud sign-in page will open (see Figure 15.18).

Figure 15.18

The iCloud sign-in page.

2. Enter your Apple ID and password information in the appropriate fields and click the Sign-In arrow icon. The iCloud home page will open (see Figure 15.19).

Figure 15.19

The iCloud home page.

3. Click one of the options. That page will appear with the information from all of your iCloud devices. Figure 15.20 displays sample content when the iWork icon is selected.

Figure 15.20

View iPad documents online at any time.

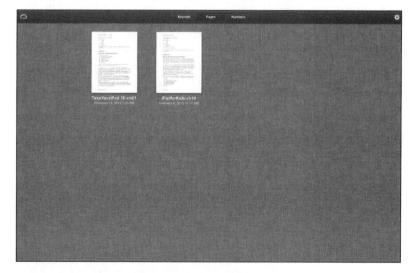

Back Up Your iPad to iCloud

One of the major changes brought to the iPad since it was first released is the capability to, if users so choose, never to have to be connected to an iTunes-enabled computer again. While many users can and do connect their iPads to a computer to back up their information, they can now skip this step and back up directly to iCloud.

Why do this? Because bad things, unfortunately, will happen. You could drop your iPad, or lose it. Or have it, sadly, stolen. If any of these events were to happen, you would have to reconstruct all your information from scratch. But, if you back your iPad up, you can have all your information (including your apps) back in minutes.

By default, Apple provides every iCloud user with 5GB of space within iCloud to store information from the iPad (or any other iOS device) with the option to buy more storage on an annual basis.

To back up your iPad to iCloud:

1. Tap the Settings app icon. The Settings app will open.
2. Tap the iCloud settings option. The iCloud settings pane will appear.
3. Tap the Storage & Backup option. The Storage & Backup pane will open (see Figure 15.21).

Figure 15.21

Configuring online backup options.

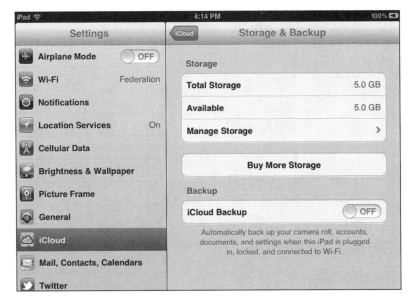

4. Slide the iCloud Backup setting to On. A Start iCloud Backup dialog will appear.
5. Tap OK. The dialog will close, and a new Back Up Now button will appear.
6. Tap the Back Up Now button. The backup process will start (see Figure 15.22).

Figure 15.22

Backing up your iPad.

It is quite possible, as time goes on, that the amount of data on your iPad will grow too large to be stored on 5GB of storage. If that happens, you can purchase more storage on an annual subscription basis.

First, you should see if you are even near the point where you have to buy more storage.

To manage storage use on iCloud:

1. In the Storage & Backup pane of the iCloud settings page, tap the Manage Storage option. The Manage Storage pane will appear, shown in Figure 15.23.

2. If you want to see exactly what files are being stored by each iCloud-enabled app listed, tap the app in question. The list of files will be displayed.

3. To manage individual files, tap the Edit button. The Edit screen will appear, as shown in Figure 15.24.

Figure 15.23

Managing the iPad's storage.

Figure 15.24

Pick and choose what files to keep.

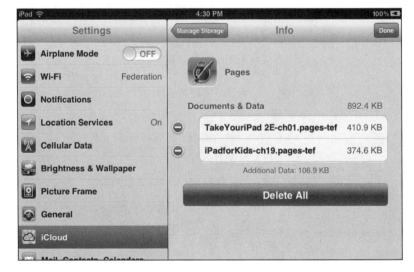

4. Tap one of the files' Delete buttons to select the file for removal or tap the Delete All button. A confirmation dialog will be displayed.

5. Tap the Delete button. The file(s) will be removed.

6. Tap Done. The Edit pane will close.

To purchase more storage for backing up in iCloud:

1. On either the Manage Storage or Storage & Backup pane, tap the Buy More Storage button. The Buy More Storage action dialog will open, as seen in Figure 15.25.

Figure 15.25

Getting more iCloud storage.

2. Tap one of the displayed Upgrade options. The option will be selected.

3. Tap the Buy button. The Apple ID verification dialog will appear.

4. Enter your Apple ID password and tap OK. The amount will be billed to your iTunes account, and the new storage will be made available to your iCloud account.

Securing Your iPad

Since the iPad is a mobile device, it makes sense that you would have it with you on the road, away from your home. It also makes sense that you may have left it somewhere and forgotten where it is. Or worse, someone may have walked off with it.

The good news is that you can track down your iPad using the Find My iPad tool included with iCloud. This handy tool will let you track down the location of your iPad based on cellular triangulation or known WiFi network locations, so you can get an idea of where the device might be, as long as it is on and connected to the Internet.

To locate the iPad, log into the iCloud site and navigate to the Find My iPhone page. After you log in again, click the Find option. In a few moments, the location of your iPad will be displayed on a map (see Figure 15.26).

Figure 15.26

iPad missing?
Not for long.

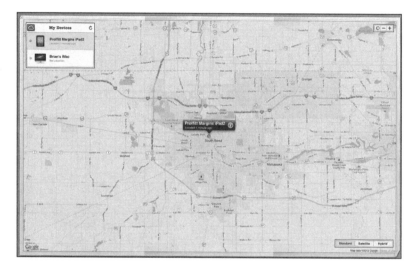

If you suspect the device was left in a public place, you can have the device start making noise and display a message to whomever might find it. You may be pleasantly surprised by the kindness of strangers.

Once the iPad is located, click the blue information icon on the location placard. The placard will expand to reveal more options (see Figure 15.27).

Click the Play Sound or Send Message button to open a message editor window. Enter a short message to whomever finds the iPad and click Send. The message will be sent (see Figure 15.28).

Figure 15.27

More options to deal with a lost iPad.

Figure 15.28

Broadcast for help.

> **NOTE**   **Talking to Strangers**
>
> Always be careful and don't send out too much contact information on the alert message. A phone number is usually enough. If someone calls back, always arrange to meet that person at a public place to retrieve your iPad device. I recommend the local police station or somewhere very conspicuous.

Alas, you may have lost the iPad to someone with nefarious intentions. You have two options when that happens. First, you can lock the iPad remotely with a numeric password that will render the iPad unusable until the password is entered. Just click the Remote Lock option and follow the onscreen instructions. Once you click Lock, the iPad will only unlock when the four-digit number is entered (see Figure 15.29).

Figure 15.29

Lock the iPad up.

If you have sensitive data on your iPad (and any personal contact information would qualify), you may want to take the more drastic measure of Remote Wipe, which will immediately reset the iPad to factory condition. You should only take this option if you are sure the device has been stolen or is otherwise irretrievable, because restoring the system's data if the device is ever recovered will take some time, and you will no longer be able to track the iPad.

Conclusion

Now that you are ready to travel, you will find the iPad an invaluable companion. Not only can it help get you where you are going, but it can also access your personal collection of data wherever you go.

In Chapter 16, "An iPad a Day," you'll explore a new class of apps that will help you maintain your health and nutrition and keep you fit as a fiddle.

Chapter 16
An iPad a Day

Human beings have never been as healthy as they are now. The average lifespan for men in the United States is 75.64 years, and women have it better with 80.79 years, according to the Human Mortality Database. If you really want to live longer, move to Monaco: Men live on average there to be 85.81 years old, and women have a live expectancy there of 93.90 years of age, the CIA Factbook reports.

Of course, moving to Monaco might be a bit out of reach for most of us. Better instead, perhaps, to stay where we are and work on improving our health in more traditional ways.

To say there are a lot of apps available for the iPad that can help you do this is a huge understatement: There are thousands of such apps out there right now. The reason for this is the iPhone, which came before the iPad and can run the same apps. Because the iPhone is so portable, people love to take it with them whenever they are exercising, dining out, or shopping in the grocery store.

Because of this high demand, that means there are already a rich selection of apps for you to choose from that can help you improve your general health and fitness. In this chapter, we will showcase two excellent apps to keep your body and mind running smoothly. Specifically, you will learn how to:

✳ Find useful health information with WebMD

✳ Manage your exercise routine with Fitness for iPad

The Doctor Is In

The human body is an amazingly complex system of parts, subsystems, and chemical reactions that somehow works all together in a cohesive manner to enable you to live your life.

In order to keep this system working in proper order, every once in a while you're going to need some medical help. When we were younger, visiting the doctor was a bit of a rite of passage, as you entered the examination room, endured the pokes and prods and sometimes odd questions, and left with some bad-tasting medicine and perhaps a lollipop.

Today, it would be the same experience (well, perhaps without the lollipop), except for the fact that we as a society have access to a wealth of information about health and medical issues that can help us make better and informed decisions about how our health care is to be managed.

Even better, this information is voluminous but not inaccessible: You don't have to be a nurse or a doctor in order to understand it. One of the best sources of this kind of information is WebMD, the hugely popular website that has provided medical and health information to millions of people around the world.

The WebMD app, which is free of charge, gives you access to the same information in a more interactive format. It is highly recommended for anyone interested in his or her own medical well-being.

CAUTION   Get Help Immediately

This cannot be emphasized enough: The information in WebMD is meant to be a guide, not a substitute, for actual medical treatment. Ever. Also, if you are experiencing chest pain, having difficulty breathing, bleeding severely, becoming suddenly weak or numb, or think you have any kind of medical emergency, call 911.

WebMD can help you find a variety of information in more than one useful way. In the home page displayed in Figure 16.1, you can see the tools that the app contains.

Figure 16.1

*The initial
WebMD
screen.*

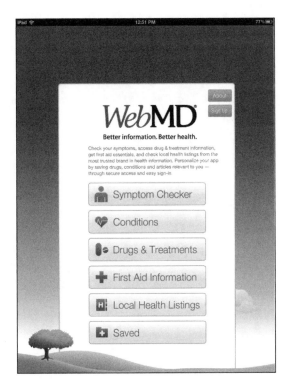

* **Symptom Checker.** An interactive map of the body that will enable you to zero in on what could possibly be bothering you.

* **Conditions.** If you or someone you know has been told they have a certain condition, you can look it up with this tool and learn more.

* **Drugs & Treatments.** Find out anything you need about medications you or a loved one might be taking, including side effects and interactions.

* **First Aid Information.** A compendium of first-aid practices.

* **Local Health Listings.** Using your current location, this tool will help you find nearby health care providers.

* **Saved.** If you have a WebMD account, you can store any information from the other tools (except Symptom Checker) in this section.

To set up a free WebMD account:

1. In the WebMD app, tap the Sign Up button on the home screen. A notification dialog will appear.

2. Tap Sign Up. The Sign Up dialog box will appear (see Figure 16.2).

Figure 16.2

Sign up for a WebMD account.

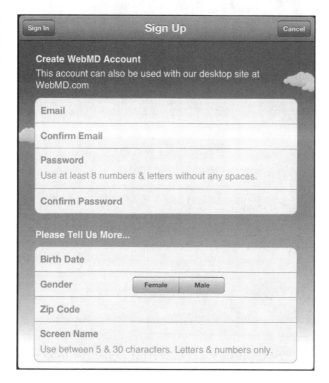

3. Type in all the requested information and tap Sign In. A notification dialog will appear, informing you that your account has been created.

4. Tap OK. The Create PIN dialog box will appear.

5. If you want a four-digit PIN to sign into the WebMD app instead of a longer password, type the PIN. The Confirm PIN screen will appear.

6. Type the PIN again. A notification dialog will inform you that your PIN has been created.

7. Tap OK. The home screen will appear again.

One of the more interesting features of the WebMD app is the Symptom Checker, which has a neat interactive map of the body that lets you pinpoint symptoms.

To use Symptom Checker:

1. In the WebMD app, tap the Symptom Checker button on the home screen. A How to Get Started dialog box will appear.

2. Tap OK. The Profile dialog box will appear (see Figure 16.3).

Figure 16.3

Specify your personal information.

3. Enter your Age, Gender, and Zip/Postal Code information, and tap Save. A graphic of the human body (in your gender) will appear.

4. Tap the area of the body where the symptom is. A pop-over menu will appear, listing possible symptoms for that part of the body (see Figure 16.4).

5. Tap the option in the pop-over menu that closely matches your symptom. Depending on the symptom selected, it will either move to the Your Symptoms section at the bottom of the screen, or the WebMD Symptom Checker will appear to ask you additional questions (see Figure 16.5).

Figure 16.4
Possible symptoms that could be bothering you.

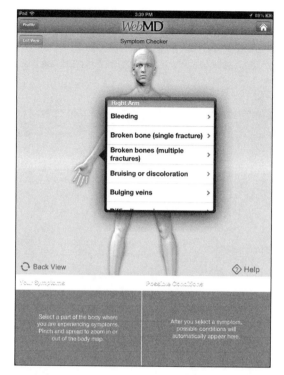

Figure 16.5
Narrowing down symptoms.

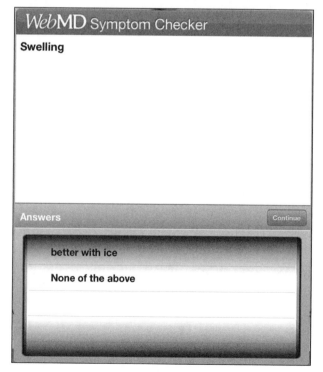

6. If presented, answer any additional questions about your symptom, tapping Continue or Next Question as needed. The symptom will appear in the Your Symptoms section.

7. If you have additional symptoms in any part of your body, continue to add them as needed.

8. Tap the Possible Conditions option you want to learn more about. Information about the condition will appear.

9. Tap another condition if you want to read about something else, or tap the Body View button to return to the human graphic.

There is a wealth of information in the WebMD app, which is constantly kept up to date. Just remember, it's there to guide your discussions with your healthcare provider and assist you in treating the minor bumps and bruises that are a part of your daily life.

Get Fit

Even as we tend to get healthier all of the time, the populations of many developed nations are struggling with the very real problem of less-than-stellar nutrition. Americans in particular have a problem with this: Our diets are very carbohydrate-heavy, which can translate to a higher than normal obesity rate.

Doctors stress that when we consume food, we need to apply (at least) a balanced approach to what we eat and how we move. If you want to keep healthy and maintain a certain weight, then you need to balance the types of food you eat with your exercise regimen.

How you do this can be wildly varied, so the Fitness for iPad app can help you discover how to do this.

The Fitness app has four primary tools, as shown in Figure 16.6.

Figure 16.6

The Fitness for iPad home screen.

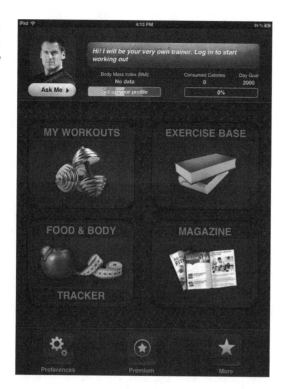

* **My Workouts.** This tool will help you construct an exercise regimen configured to your goals and comfort zone.

* **Exercise Base.** Here you will find a collection of exercises and how to do them.

* **Food & Body Tracker.** If you want to track your caloric and nutritional intake, this tool will enable you to do that. It will also let you track weight, body mass index, and other body measurements.

* **Magazine.** Premium users (those who want to pay the annual subscription fee) of the Fitness app can access additional content from Fitness magazine on a monthly or annual basis. Tap the Premium button to learn more about this feature.

Before you can use many of the features in the Fitness app, you will need to set up a profile so the app will know what content to highlight for you.

To set up a profile in Fitness:

1. In Fitness, tap the Preferences button. The Preferences action menu will appear.

2. Tap the Profile option. The Profile action menu will appear (see Figure 16.7).

Figure 16.7

Setting up a profile.

3. Type your name in the Name field and email address in the Mail field.

4. Enter the remaining information in the Profile action menu and tap outside the action menu to close the menu.

5. Tap the Body Mass Index (BMI) scale at the top of the screen. The information you entered into the profile will be calculated into a personal BMI figure and an estimated caloric intake for someone with your height, weight, and age.

After you have generated a basic profile within the Fitness app, you can then take that information and work to build an exercise regimen.

Before You Begin

Another one you've heard before, but bears repeating: Before beginning any new diet or exercise plan, discuss it with your healthcare provider.

To create a workout:

1. Tap the My Workouts button. The My Workouts screen will appear.

2. If you have no experience putting together a workout routine, tap the Personal Trainer button. The Personal Trainer screen will open (see Figure 16.8).

Figure 16.8

The Personal Trainer tool.

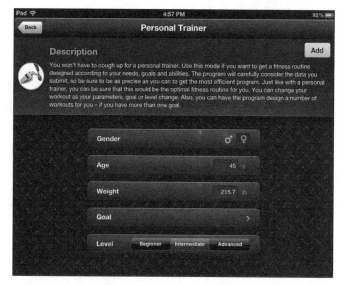

Watch Out for Add-Ons

When the Personal Trainer option is first opened, you may see a message for a customized personal trainer session on the screen. This is an advertisement for an additional (for-fee) service from Fitness, and it can be ignored.

3. If you have already done your profile, some of the information will be on the screen. Enter the additional Goal and Level information.

4. Tap the Add button. A personal exercise regimen will be generated.

There are a lot of features within the Fitness app that can keep track of what you're eating and how to monitor your progress moving toward a particular health goal. It's a great app to use for fitness tuning, no matter what age.

Conclusion

Health is the most important thing you have, of course, but there's no denying that it's also nice to have a good handle on your financial situation.

In Chapter 17, "Managing Your Money," we'll look at apps that can help you do exactly that: Get your current finances organized and plan for your retirement future.

Chapter 17
Managing Your Money

Money. We like to have it around, but unless we are really smart about it, it really likes to leave us.

The problem with money, in all seriousness, is that we live in a world where it's very easy to spend it and lose track of where we're spending it. We can spend $2.50 on a cup of coffee on a daily basis and think that this isn't too much to spend, really. But if you did that every weekday for a year, it would add up to $650 (before sales tax)!

It is a matter, then, of small picture versus big picture. In the day-to-day small picture, things don't seem to be all that expensive, but if we look at the big picture, then it becomes a little easier to spot expenditures in our lives that perhaps we can remove or replace with less-expensive alternatives.

This is exactly what apps to manage money on the iPad do: track the daily stuff and then let you step back and see the bigger picture so you can make more informed decisions about that ever-elusive money.

There are a wealth of money-managing apps that are available for the iPad, but by far the best popular personal finance app is the Mint.com app, which enables you to track daily expenditures, bank and credit card accounts, and loan and investment information. You can even use it to pay your bills online.

In this chapter, you will find out how to use these apps to:

❋ Set up a Mint.com account
❋ Manage transactions with Mint.com
❋ Track your budget with Mint.com

Online Banking Made Easy

Let's talk about online banking.

The media is flooded with stories warning you of the dangers of doing your financial business online. It may conjure up images of online criminals pushing buttons in a dark, secluded basement hideaway and instantly draining your life savings away or racking up credit card transactions and completely killing your credit rating.

In actuality, this is not something that happens very often, and on the very rare occasion it does, it's not usually the case of someone electronically breaking into the bank. Instead, it's going to be someone who has obtained your personal information through some other means and then used that information to log in to your accounts as if they were you.

There are, sadly, many ways a malicious individual can find your password and login information: the biggest one is just asking you for it. This may seem too easy, but many is the time a hacker might call you on the phone, claim he or she is from your bank and say that they need to test your account's security and to do so they need your password. This is a social engineering technique known as *phishing*, and it can also come across as an email.

Don't believe them. The bank already has access to check your account. Why wouldn't they? Anyone who claims otherwise is lying. No one needs your account number, password, or Social Security/Social Insurance number to do any sort of business with you. Ever.

Other ways you can keep yourself secure include the following:

❋ **Don't use your iPad to connect to your bank unless you are on a secure network.** That means a network where you had to use a password to start doing anything. Better instead to use it at home, where you should always have a secure network.

CAUTION **Wi-Fi No-Nos**

There is an exception to the secured Wi-Fi rule that I personally recommend: never perform any financial (or any other private) transactions in a hotel. Even if you used a password to connect with the hotel's network, sadly there are too many hotels and motels whose systems have been compromised by expert hackers or even disgruntled employees.

TIP **Not Sure How Secure?**

If you don't know how secure your home network is, here's an easy test. If you used a password to connect to your home Wi-Fi network, you're likely secure. If you don't remember, open the Settings app on your iPad, tap the Wi-Fi setting, and look at the Network to which your iPad is connected. If there's a little padlock icon next to the network name, this is a secure connection. If it's not secure, see your Internet provider to find out how to get the network secure.

* **Make sure you use a good password.** Very often, too many people use their spouse's name or their own birth date as a password, which are easy to guess. Or, worse, something very simple like "1234." If you want to pick something hard, try a combination of personal information only you would know, such as the street number of your childhood home and the last name of your favorite teacher in school.

* **Buy a shredder.** Again, it's often the non-electronic methods that give criminals access to your accounts. People can and will rifle through your trash and find useful bits of information on banking and credit card statements.

If you follow these simple guidelines, your online banking experience will be a much safer one. Using these best practices for security, let's explore how to use the Mint.com app to manage your personal finances.

Mint.com may seem too cutesy of a name for a trusted financial management company, but the online personal finance website is a hugely successful and trusted company, thanks to the easy interface it has to access your finances on the website and in the iPad app. In fact, Mint.com is so good that Intuit, makers of the venerable Quicken and QuickBooks computer applications, bought the company and used Mint.com to replace Intuit's existing Quicken Online services.

When you use the Mint.com app, the very first thing you must do is create a Mint.com account.

TIP   Before You Begin

Before you set up your Mint.com account, make sure that you have a good password in mind for the Mint.com account. Also, make sure that your bank or credit union has online access available and that you have a login and password for getting to your financial institution's website. If you don't have such access, contact your bank or credit union to have that set up.

To set up a Mint.com account:

1. Tap the Mint.com app. The first time you use it, the Welcome screen will appear.
2. Tap the Sign Up for Free button. The New to Mint? Screen will open (see Figure 17.1).
3. Type the information into the fields on the screen and tap the Sign Up for Free button again. The Add Account dialog box will appear (see Figure 17.2).
4. If you don't see the name of your financial institution in the first list, type the name of your institution in the Search bar. Your institution should appear in the All Results list.

Figure 17.1

The New to Mint? screen.

Figure 17.2

Add a financial account to your Mint.com account.

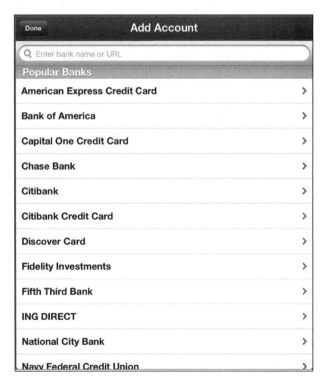

> ## TIP   My Financial Institution Is Missing
>
> If you can't find your bank or credit union, make sure that you have the full name of the institution. If you still can't find it, contact your bank and see if they have enabled Mint.com access to their online banking system.

5. Tap the name of your financial institution. The login screen for your financial institution will appear.

6. Enter the login and password for your financial institution and tap the Add it! button. The connection will be established, and your recent transactions downloaded. (Be aware that this could take a while.) Once the account is downloaded, a dialog box asking to add an additional account will appear.

> ## NOTE   Establishing Your Identity
>
> If your financial institution has additional steps to establish your online identity (such as providing your mother's maiden name or childhood pet's name), you may have to enter this information within the Add Account dialog to complete the connection.

7. If you want to add more accounts, tap Sure. Otherwise, tap Later. The Mint.com home screen will appear (see Figure 17.3).

You can add as many accounts as you want to the Mint.com account, though only bank and credit card-type accounts. Mint.com will also help you track your loan, investment, and real estate information, but this information has to (for now) be entered on the Mint.com site using a browser connection.

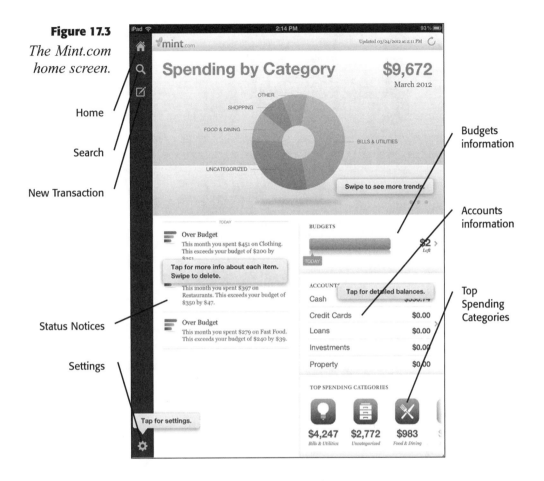

Figure 17.3
*The Mint.com
home screen.*

Home

Search

New Transaction

Status Notices

Settings

Budgets
information

Accounts
information

Top
Spending
Categories

What the Mint.com app will enable you to do is view and edit all
of your transactions and even enter new ones.

To add a new transaction (such as a cash purchase):

1. In the Mint.com app, tap the New Transaction icon. The Add
   Transaction action menu will appear (see Figure 17.4).

NOTE   Where Are You?

The first time you add a transaction, you will be asked if you
want Mint.com to use the iPad's location services. If you
choose to do this, then when you add a transaction at the
actual place for the transaction, the merchant's name
should come up in the Choose a Merchant field or list.

Figure 17.4

Adding a transaction.

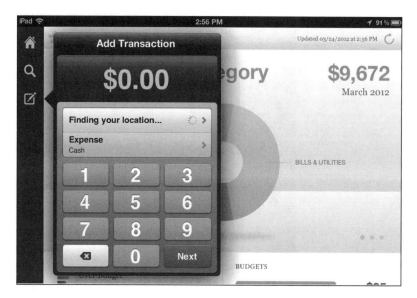

2. Type the amount of the transaction. The transaction will appear as a negative value.

3. If a merchant is not visible in the Choose a merchant field, tap the field. The Choose Merchant action menu will appear.

4. Tap the merchant if they are on the Local list, or type the merchant's name in the Enter Merchant Name bar. The Add Transaction action menu will reappear.

5. Tap the Expense field. The Transaction Type action menu will appear (see Figure 17.5).

6. Tap the Cash Payment Type option.

7. Slide the Split from last ATM setting to On. This is useful if you are using cash you withdrew from an ATM.

8. Tap the Back button. The Add Transaction action menu will reappear.

9. Tap Next. The review pane will appear on the menu (see Figure 17.6).

10. If you want to set a category for this transaction, tap the Category field. The Category action menu will appear.

11. Scroll down the list to find the appropriate category or enter the category name in the Search bar.

Figure 17.5

Determine the Transaction Type.

Figure 17.5

Determine the Transaction Type.

Figure 17.6

Review your transaction.

Figure 17.6

Review your transaction.

12. Tap the category name in the list and tap the Save button. The Add Transaction review action menu will reappear.

13. Tap Done. The transaction will be entered into Mint.com.

When Mint.com imports your banking information from your financial institution, it may not assign a category to every transaction. If you are not using Mint.com to track your budget, this is not a big deal, but in order to accurately monitor your expenses, you should make sure that each transaction has a category assigned.

To edit any uncategorized transactions:

1. In the Top Spending Categories section of the home screen, scroll to the Uncategorized listings and tap it. A chart of all uncategorized transactions will appear (see Figure 17.7).

Figure 17.7

View transactions by Category, even uncategorized ones.

2. Tap the number of transactions button. The Transactions screen will appear.

3. Tap one of the transaction listings. The listing's information pane will slide out (see Figure 17.8).

Figure 17.8

*A
transaction's
information
pane.*

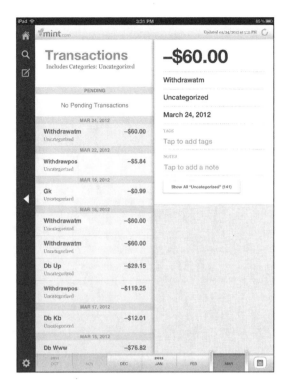

4. Tap the Uncategorized category. The Category action menu will appear.

5. Find the appropriate category or enter the category name in the Search bar.

6. Tap the category name in the list. The new category will be applied.

7. Repeat steps 3–6 as needed until all the uncategorized transactions are properly organized.

Although you can't create or edit a budget on the Mint.com app (you have to use the Mint.com website to do that for now), you can instantly see in what areas you need to reduce your spending or where you may have gone over budget.

Tap the Budgets section of the home screen to view the Budget screen (see Figure 17.9).

Figure 17.9

The Budget screen.

Today's date

On this screen, you can immediately see where you might be facing some issues. The Today's date indicator shows how far in the month you have left to go, percentage-wise. So, in this example budget, even though the Gas & Fuel budget category still shows some money left, it's still past the line of where it should be at this point in the month. Which means, based on projected spending, I would need to be careful and watch my spending in this category.

Conclusion

Whether it's managing your money, taking care of your health, or communicating with the ones you love, the iPad is an extremely versatile device for baby boomers to use. In this book, we have shown you just some of the great ways the iPad can assist you, without all of the headache and hassle of a more complicated computer.

Using the techniques and skills you have learned in this book, you should feel confident about exploring some of the thousands of apps that are available for the iPad. With new apps and tools coming out every day, you can make the iPad your own personal assistant that can free up your time and help enrich your world.

Index